SEASHELL PARADE

(Frontispiece). *Lambis crocata pilsbryi* Abbott. Photograph by Daniel Boust

SEASHELL PARADE

FASCINATING FACTS, PICTURES, AND STORIES

by A. Gordon Melvin, Ph.D.

~~~~~~

CHARLES E. TUTTLE COMPANY

Rutland • Vermont: Tokyo • Japan

Representatives

For Continental Europe:
BOXERBOOKS, INC., *Zurich*
For the British Isles:
PRENTICE-HALL INTERNATIONAL, INC., *London*
For Canada:
M. G. HURTIG, LTD., *Edmonton*

Published by the Charles E. Tuttle Company, Inc.
of Rutland, Vermont & Tokyo, Japan
with editorial offices at
Suido 1-chome, 2-6, Bunkyo-ku, Tokyo

Copyright in Japan, 1973
by A. Gordon Melvin

Library of Congress Catalog Card No. 72-96776
International Standard Book No. 0-8048 0971-2

First printing, 1973

PRINTED IN JAPAN

TO MY WIFE

LORNA

A TRIBUTE

TABLE OF CONTENTS

PERSONAL NOTE

APPRECIATION IS DUE TO MY WIFE LORNA, WHOSE *behind-the-scenes aid has helped me avoid many errors. Most of the best photographs are hers. I am grateful to Pearl Ann Reeder, editor of* Hobbies, *who willingly arranged for my use of materials, most of which appeared in that magazine. The contents of this book have been selected in terms of what I hope may be interesting to shell collectors. Since I alone am responsible for the accuracy of what is written here I offer my apologies for my shortcomings.*

—A. GORDON MELVIN

ABOUT THIS BOOK

MOST PEOPLE LIKE TO READ ABOUT THINGS IN WHICH they are interested. This book is addressed to those who enjoy reading about shells. It might be thought of as a series of one-way conversations meant to supply information, some of it practical and some merely curious, on this subject. The book has no serious purpose, and those who regard themselves highly as scholars or critics should pass it by.

Unlike my earlier *Sea Shells of the World with Values,* this book is not primarily concerned with shell portrayal and identification. The illustrations are intended to be topical; most of them are no more than pictorial introductions to what follows.

The title *Seashell Parade* is a frank attempt to avoid overworked titles of the past. Few realize how very many shell books have been published, off and on, during the last three hundred years. In the last decade, especially, books on shells have been coming from the presses with increasing frequency, bearing titles that have echoed other titles, past and recent. If this present title avoids confusion with earlier ones, it will have served its purpose.

LATIN OR ENGLISH?

Since they are the only universal names, the Latin scientific ones frequently occur here. Many readers who have long been familiar with Latin names will take them as a matter of course. In recent years, however, the classical languages have been less and less taught in schools, so that many high school and college graduates, even those who have become scientists, know little Latin. Nevertheless, they learn Latin words as easily as new English ones, since Latin names are no more difficult to learn than those other new words we are always adding to our vocabularies, like *astronaut* and *ecology*. The common Deep Sea Scallop has the scientific name of *Pecten magellanicus*. Yet *scallop* would seem to be just as peculiar a word as *magellanicus*.

The apprehension of some shell lovers concerning Latin names seems to stem from the fear that they will not be able to pronounce these names correctly. There is not much to worry about on that score. In fact, there are several different systems of pronunciation in use in universities, while none is known to have been actually used by the ancient Romans. A Mexican shell collector and I use two very different systems, mine learned in a Canadian university and his in a Mexican one. When we use the Latin names of shells we have agreed to differ amicably, each pronouncing them in his own way.

Collectors sometimes have a feeling of attachment to such common shell-names as Angel Wing and Jingle Shell. Such names are descriptive and comfortably familiar. One does not continue long with shells, however, without discovering that perhaps three-quarters of them have no common names at all. The only names they bear are Latin ones that are often hard to translate. (The name *Epitonium scalare,* for example, is almost untranslatable, though the word *scalare* may be translated as "staircase." The common name of this lovely shell, however, bears little relation to the Latin, being widely established as Precious Wentletrap.) In the long run, common names will not do. Is it not wise to face the fact that the best name is the Latin one? After that, if there is a common name, it is easy to remember it also.

A FAMILY OF FRIENDS

Readers of these pages are probably shell collectors or candidates for such a preoccupation. To own one shell, perhaps a tiger cowry or a pink-stained queen conch, is a satisfaction. But, as one swallow does not make a summer, so one shell does not make a collection. When once an interest in shells has been awakened, there may be a strong push to go on to the making of a small or a larger collection, to find in shells a short-time solace or a lifetime diversion.

There are all kinds of collectors. Children often collect shells because they are eager beings; those who are older do so because their sensibilities have remained alive. To some the matter is a hobby. Others are wholesomely acquisitive. Some, of artistic leanings, are fascinated by the beauty of shells, seeking lovely form and color.

All such activity is doubtless good, if only because to do something is always better than not to do anything. There is a wide camaraderie among shell fanciers, and membership in this family is free and easy. There is no need to feel inferior in the presence of those who have specialized scientific knowledge. In a sense, though professional malacologists are not shell collectors *per se,* they are usually found to be so friendly that they need not inspire awe. Shell collecting is not a science, but an expression of our attitudes and longings.

Those who live near the shore may make for themselves a local collection. Soon they pass the limits of the locality and must travel elsewhere or exchange with others. Since they cannot travel to all the shores of all the continents they must buy shells,* or exchange their treasures with other local collectors or with those who live on distant shores.

Working with shells is a tremendous stimulus to activity, physical, mental, and social. You may be led outdoors into a search along the shore, or into a trip to

* The current list of one seller of shells may be obtained by sending a request, with a stamped, self-addressed envelope, to the author at 863 Watertown St., West Newton, Mass. 02165.

the Florida Keys, the coast of Western Mexico or the Great Barrier Reef. On the other hand, there is plenty to do indoors, classifying, labeling, and organizing your collection. You may pore over books on shells. You may correspond with collectors in far places or meet with those who live nearby. Few avocations lead so directly to the making of worthwhile friends.

In any case, you are your own seeker on your own path, a path which may merely lead you along the seashore or into the depths of philosophy. If you continue in your quest you will inevitably ask fundamental questions as to the *how* and the *why*. The true answers to such queries, if you find them, can hardly fail to make you a wiser and happier person.

SHELLS WITH A STORY

1. MYSTERY SHELL:
THE NAUTILUS

What is probably the world's all-time favorite among seashells, the Chambered Nautilus, *Nautilus pompilius* L., is the shell of a mollusk which, after thousands of years of human notice, still remains something of a mystery. The shell itself is neither scarce nor harder than usual to obtain. It has all the characteristics that make it desired by shell collectors, decorators, artists, and just plain people.

It is large. Its curves are little short of magnificent. In form it approximates the mathematician's "logarithmic spiral." It has color, black and brown painted against white, is pearly inside, and, if treated with acid, becomes pearly all over; it is then called the Pearly Nautilus.

Most astonishing of all, it is built up inside with a series of lunules, or chambers, which present an even more amazing appearance of spiral beauty. Almost as much wanted as the whole shell are the split halves which show the chambers. These are connected by a hollow middle cord, or siphuncle, by means of which the animal keeps in touch with the empty chambers. As each chamber is left behind, it is sealed off, and the animal grows into a new and larger chamber. At the mouth of the shell the animal lives, and moves, and has its predatory being, on the deep sea bottom of tropical Pacific seas.

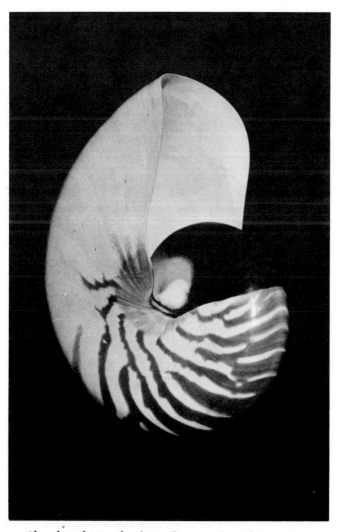

1. Chambered Nautilus (*Nautilus pompilius L.*)

The mystery is connected with the chambers and the fine tube which connects them. Aristotle described (and perhaps named) the Nautilus, or "little sailor," and associated it with another shell, the Paper Nautilus, which resembles it only slightly. For two thousand years the subject lay still until, about a hundred years ago, it caused something of a scientific sensation in Europe because of arguments about its way of life. Since then continuous publicity has made the Nautilus the world's best-known shell.

Recently, I tried to record some important writings about the Nautilus on a tape, but gave up after filling an 1800-foot reel. Much that is written concerns the century-old squabble as to whether the Nautilus can actually rise and sink at will, making it Nature's own submarine. Some reports claim that the Nautilus merely crawls the sea bottom shell-hump up, made balloon-like by gas in the inner chambers. There it roams, feeding on crabs and choice sea-morsels. Others claim that the compressed air mechanism, made possible by muscle, siphon, and gas chambers found to contain nitrogen, enables the animal to sink or swim.* In any case, the name Nautilus has been given to a series of United States submarines, including the latest atomic masterpiece.

Furthermore, Oliver Wendell Holmes, in his famed poem "The Chambered Nautilus," made the shell a symbol of human aspiration because of its manner of always living in a wider and fuller way, with a new and larger chamber for each period of its life.

* Later undersea photography has shown the Nautilus to be a free-swimming inhabitant of the deeps, rising and falling as it contracts its inner gas chambers.

In the way in which it is interlocked with human action and human life, the Nautilus is fabulous. Plentiful today in the seas south of the Philippines, in the Sulu Sea, and the vicinity of Fiji and the New Hebrides, it is fished for by natives, mostly in the early summer. Bamboo traps are baited, strung on ropes, and sunk into the depths. A plentiful catch usually follows. Some of it is sold in the local market for food, but thousands of shells are cleaned and sent to such clearing centers as Zamboanga and Manila. From there great cases of the shells are shipped to many parts of the world, for the making of pearl ornaments, and for the delight of thousands of people who never cease to be charmed by the superb dignity and symbolic grandeur of the magnificent Nautilus.

The shell itself may be stood up in any way in a collection. It may be set up on end, vaselike, by attaching four small snails as feet, using household-type cement. It may also be displayed "natural," or in its pearly form, or as split halves. Mine is divided and set on a teakwood stand I once bought in China. There it stands, continually recalling its old mystery for, oddly enough, science has never yet told us whether it can actually sink and surface at will.

Until we have the answer, we may cherish the hope that, when the actual truth at last is known, the Nautilus will be found to have the unusual powers ascribed to it. In any case, the Nautilus will always be a Mystery Shell, for it still presents, to all generations of men, the mystery of its superb and elusive beauty.

2. GLORY OF THE SEA

The highly prized seashell Glory of the Sea is so much coveted that, lacking a specimen, my friend the brilliant artist and shell collector Ethlyn Woodlock made a model of it in wood, and painted it to life. This shell is so rare that even a photograph of it has been hard to come by, and until recently the only photograph I had seen of Glory of the Sea was that of the noted specimen in the American Museum of Natural History in New York.

A few months ago it seemed I should have an opportunity, for the first time, to see a newly discovered specimen of this shell, which is scientifically named *Conus gloriamaris* Chemnitz. A collector, just in from the Marshall Islands, telephoned saying he had brought with him a new specimen of what he believed to be the Glory of the Sea, and that he would bring it in to show me.

When he arrived, the specimen he brought me did look like the famous shell. But my wife detected certain variations which prompted her to take it in the Museum of Comparative Zoology at Harvard for study and possible verification of identity. To the chagrin of the owner, the shell turned out to be a *Conus aureus* Hwass, a beautiful shell worth about twenty-five dollars (all prices in U.S. dollars).

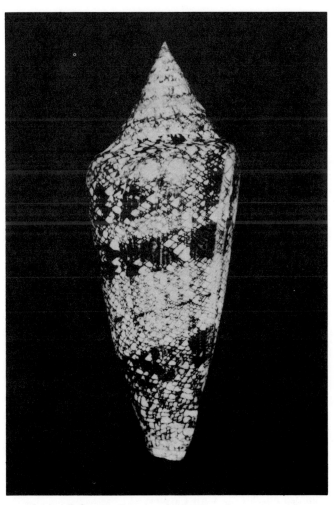

2. Glory of the Sea (*Conus gloriamaris* Chemnitz). Solomon Islands Type.

Conus gloriamaris somewhat resembles another tented cone, the common but decorative *Conus textile,* or Cloth-of-Gold Cone, which is found in most collections.

Hopeful collectors, seeing the charm of Glory of the Sea, sometimes write eager inquiries. But there is small chance of accidentally running across a *Conus gloriamaris,* since most specimens become famous on discovery, and their whereabouts and owners are known. A note has just come in that a new specimen has been acquired by the Santa Barbara Museum in California.

There are quite a few reports and stories told and written about Glory of the Sea, too much to cover in full. I quote a definitive book,* *Cone Shells of the World* (1964), by A. F. Marsh and O. H. Rippingale: "This species, while not the most beautiful in the family, is nevertheless the most glamorous. Every collector dreams of owning a specimen, and some fortunate few may realize this dream in the coming years. Good luck to them."

Mistaken identity is a common problem with sea-shells. We frequently get a letter or a visit from some collector who optimistically believes he has had a stroke of luck in obtaining an unusual shell that will net him a good sum of money. A large specimen of the Carnelian Cowry, for instance, may be confused with the Golden Cowry, which it slightly resembles. One gentleman wrote to say he believed he had the very rare *Cypraea leucodon*, reputed to be worth fifteen hundred dollars. But his shell turned out to be the ordinary though beautiful *Cypraea vitellus*, or Calf Cowry.

* For more information on this book, and other shell publications mentioned in this volume, see Chapter 74.

From its knock-out name, Glory of the Sea, one might be inclined to believe that this famed "cone" (as shells of the genus *Conus* are called), is exceedingly beautiful. It is lovely, but there are dozens of other shells which most people would consider more attractive in appearance. The halo of *Conus gloriamaris* is rather due to a legendary glamour that has grown up about this shell, partly because of its grandiose name. Just as the name Golden Cowry has endowed that shell with a fame out of proportion to its rarity, so the name Glory of the Sea has led folk in general to talk and write about it continually and frequently. This fame has been advanced by the recent discovery of several new specimens, accompanied by publicity, and also by a remark, attributed to an owner, that he would not part with his specimen for a thousand dollars.

3. MORE ABOUT
GLORY OF THE SEA

There will probably always be eager individuals with a belief in their good luck who think they have, fresh-caught or in their collections, prize shells hitherto unrecognized. A hopeful correspondent who had just seen a photograph of *Conus gloriamaris* wrote me recently offering to sell me two specimens that he was sure were Glory of the Sea. Hesitatingly I asked him to send a photograph so we could make a check. When photographs of the two shells arrived they showed two specimens of the very common though attractive Olive Shell.

Each year now, new reports come in of fresh specimens newly caught. It is rumored that skin divers have located the breeding place of this shell and are finding quite a few new specimens. But, if this is true, they are being craftily held back, as rare shells have been before, to keep up the price. One of the new specimens currently reported is said to have been secured by Bob Atkinson in Rabaul. It is claimed that this is the finest specimen that has come from the New Guinea area. I understand that he purchased it on the south coast of New Guinea for a small sum, but has been offered a thousand dollars for it.

S. Peter Dance, in his 1966 illustrated history, *Shell Collecting,* has selected four shells for special notice as

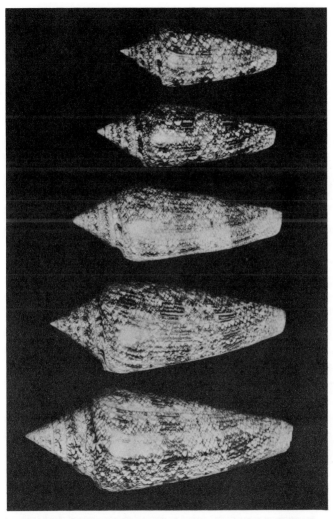

3. Growth Series of *Conus gloriamaris* Chemnitz. Collection of Ernesto Santos Galindo.

famous rarities. The shells he has chosen for this special acclaim are the Precious Wentletrap, the Matchless Cone (*Conus cedonulli*), the Glassy Nautilus, and the Glory of the Sea. On the latter he gives fresh, interesting information, in an account that is probably the most complete on record, listing the approximately fifty known specimens according to the dates they were recorded and giving for each its size, locality of discovery, history, and probable whereabouts. Dance's book reveals that *Conus gloriamaris* has had a written history, kept by many, for over two hundred years, right down to the present. Many of the great names in shell history are associated with it, and it has been present in some of the world's most distinguished collections.

The earliest record is found in a sales catalogue of 1757 which mentions a specimen owned by a Dutchman named Schluyter. This very shell was sold to A. G. Moltke, who lent it to the famous Danish collector Johann Chemnitz. Chemnitz described it and published his account with an illustration in 1777. Specimens have been owned by such distinguished collectors as Sowerby, Reeve, Cuming, and Hwass (for more information on these men, see Conchology's Hall of Fame, pp. 337–58); specimens of *Conus gloriamaris* have also had a place in the Tankerville Collection. Some are owned by the Leyden Natural History Museum, and some by the British Museum. A specimen was reported stolen from the American Museum of Natural History in New York, but the tale is said to have involved a mistake and so is probably false.

For about two hundred years the natural habitat of Glory of the Sea seems to have been unknown. The great shell explorer, Hugh Cuming, set out for remote parts of the Philippines in 1836 to make a shell study and survey of this rich area. He yearned to achieve the seemingly hopeless task of finding a specimen of *Conus gloriamaris* for himself. After he had spent years in such explorations, to his utter amazement he turned over a stone one day and found two specimens. Even though they were poor and immature ones, it was a wonderful discovery. At the time he was hunting for shells on a reef at Jacna, Bohol Island, and is reported to have almost fainted with delight.

This discovery gave some vague notion of where these shells actually live. But they continued to be rare and virtually unobtainable. An American paid as much as two thousand dollars for one specimen.

The shell remained almost unobtainable for such a long time because its true breeding area was not really known. Recently, however, a number of specimens have been discovered near New Guinea and New Britain. Thus the *Conus gloriamaris* shell, once so rare, is now perhaps less rare than some others of less glamour. The *Hawaiian Shell News,* published in Honolulu, keeps collectors posted on everything new about Glory of the Sea, a shell which will always be one of the most talked about (and written about) of all the shells of the sea.

4. THE TRITON

The Triton Shell is one of those universal shell favorites popular on its own merits. It is displayed not only by collectors but by many who, owning no other shell, are struck by the decorative effect of this one.

It is much prized for its looks—its large size, the plump rounding of its body whorl, its gracefully tapering spire, and its waving pattern of deep brown on cream, resembling a rich fabric.

The shell comes from deep South Pacific waters and is found in ocean areas extending roughly from the Philippines toward Fiji and Northern Australia. Caught by fishermen, it is sent all over the world, for it has countless admirers in every land.

Specimens vary considerably in size. The smaller ones have a special charm because of their glistening surfaces and their perfect form. The more coveted large specimens may be a foot or more in length. Having remained a long time in the deep sea, they become a bit roughened in their battle with the environment, and the tips of their spires are almost always broken off.

Furthermore, because of the careless handling and packing of many native shippers, the shells often arrive chipped or broken. More than once I have been dismayed to unpack a box of these lovely shells and find a frill

4. Triton Shell (*Cymatium tritonis*; also called *Charonia tritonis*).

broken off, or worse still, a huge hole crushed into the body. Large, perfect shells are hard to come by.

The common name of this shell, the Triton, comes from the demigod of that name who, in classical mythology, is the son of Neptune and Amphitrite. Triton was formed as a merman; the lower half of his body was like the body of a fish. He is pictured blowing this particular shell as his trumpet, and in fact it was his duty, we are told, to blow this trumpet when Neptune decided it was time to rustle up a storm.

Once upon a time the scientific name of this shell was *Cymatium tritonis* L., hence its common name of Triton. It is only one of a large number of shells of the genus *Cymatium,* a word which means "a wave," presumably an allusion to the wavelike markings on some of these shells. There has, however, been much name-changing affecting this shell, and although older books give it the name *Cymatium tritonis*, some more recent ones list it as a *Cymatium* called *Charonia tritonis*.

There is a shell found off the East Coast of the United States, in the waters about southeastern Florida and the West Indies, which resembles *tritonis* so closely that it is hard to distinguish between them. An obvious difference, however, is that adult specimens of the West Indies shell have a swollen angular shoulder on the last whorl.

In the Harvard publication Johnsonia, a series edited by Dr. William Clench (vols. 35–36), this latter shell is called *Charonia variegata* Lam. But in his magnificent book, *Sea Shells of North America* (1968), Dr. R. Tucker Abbott calls it by its more usual name of *Charonia nobilis* Conrad. Label it one or all, as you like, I stick to *nobilis*.

The long generations of human beings who have admired, exhibited, and used *nobilis* have cared little about its name. A more mundane approach has been shown to it by using it as a trumpet. Large shells of many species have always been used by ancient peoples as trumpets. The Aztecs of Mexico used large *Muricidae* and the temple worshipers of India used the Sacred Chank.

In the tropical countries of the Pacific, the grand trumpet of them all has been, from time immemorial and to this day, the large Triton Shell. Every so often you catch a glimpse of it being blown in some television documentary or moving picture. Recently one of these showed it used in the colorful pageant of a Christian festival procession on the island of Madeira. A photo of Japanese priests blowing this shell is in the famous sea-shell number of the *National Geographic Magazine* (July, 1949).

A classic example of the shell itself may be seen in what is perhaps the world's greatest repository of shells, the British Museum, London. It is a ceremonial shell, taken long ago from the mouth of the Fly River, New Guinea, where it was used to ward off evil spirits from a village.

Curious and enterprising persons today still like the trumpet form for their specimens. In fact, one ingenious friend told me that, when he received a shipment of partly broken Tritons, he made holes in them to turn them into trumpets. Such a trumpet may be made in either of two ways: by making a mouthpiece at the tip, or by cutting a hole in the side of one whorl near the top of the spire. The trumpet's mellow note cannot but gladden the heart of a shell fancier who envisions himself as one of a long line of Triton blowers.

5. STORY OF THE SACRED CHANK

The unique seashell popularly known as the Sacred Chank first came to my attention some years ago when my wife and I were staying in Ceylon. There we received an invitation from an Indian friend to visit Travancore, where she entertained us and arranged an audience for us with the Maharani and Maharajah of Travancore. It was then we discovered that this unusual seashell is portrayed on the official crest of the South India State of Trivandrum. This added special interest to our visit to the towering temple where the silver-chased Chank is used in religious ceremonies.

There are a few seashells which man has selected from thousands for special attention or use. From time to time, in this book, I plan to tell the story of some of these remarkable shells. One of them is certainly this Sacred Chank, *Xancus pyrum* L., which is taken today by divers off the coast of India and Ceylon. This shell has been raised by Hindus to the status of a symbol and has even been deified. For centuries it has been an object of veneration and worship.

The reasons for this do not lie in the characteristics of the shell itself but rather in the story of the shell as found in the Hindu scriptures. This is one of the tales about the god Vishnu, second person of the Hindu trinity.

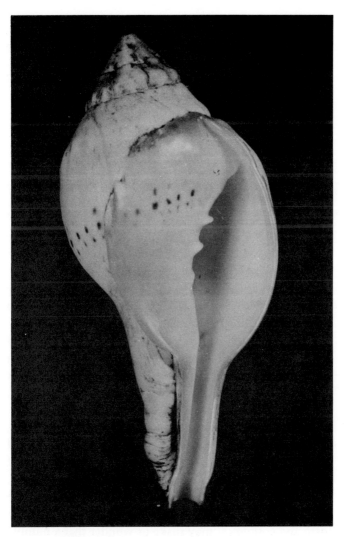

5. Sacred Chank (*Xancus pyrum* L.).

Vishnu had the special power of changing himself into any form he chose, appearing, for examples, as a fish, a bird, or a lion. When the sacred scriptures were stolen by the Chank, Vishnu became a fish, chased the Chank, and recovered the books.

The shell itself is of noble form, very thick and heavy, mature shells being about five to eight inches in length. The body whorl is globular and the canal graceful. Its internal parts are so curved that it is cut up and made into bracelets used by the women of Bengal as jewelry. The whole shell is used as a trumpet in religious ceremonies, often being decorated with brass mountings. Left-handed chanks, with the opening to the left instead of to the right, are rare. These may be chased in silver and used in temple worship.

For some years this magnificent shell was not coming into the United States, and it was seldom available to American collectors. Recently, however, my wife received a number of them from a friend in Ceylon and a promise of some more, just as soon as the ants eat out the flesh of some fresh-caught shells. Many collectors want to have a specimen of this shell because it is so famous.

In fact, a whole book has been written on the subject, *The Sacred Chank of India,* by James Hornell. This book, Madras Fisheries Bulletin 7 (1914), is unfortunately out of print, although a copy is to be found in the library of the American Museum of Natural History in New York.

In this book, if I remember correctly, is to be found the following prayer to the Sacred Chank. Novel to us, in form and content, it may make us wonder that a humble seashell could be set apart and valued so highly:

At the mouth of this shell is the God of the Moon, on its sides is Varuna, on its back Prajapait, and on its apex the Ganges, the Sarasvati, and all the other sacred rivers of the three worlds in which they make ablutions according to the command of Vasudeva. In this Chank is the Chief of the Brahmans. This is why we worship the Sacred Chank.

Glory to thee, sacred shell, blessed by all the gods, born in the sea, and formerly held by Vishnu in his hand. We adore the Sacred Chank, and meditate upon it. May we be filled with joy. I offer everything needful for worship—perfumes, rice, and flowers.

6. THE SAINT JAMES SCALLOP

Some seashells are of particular interest because they have, in some way, become entangled or associated with certain folkways. The Sacred Chank, for instance, is related to religious teachings and activities in India. The use of the Quahog Clam as money, in early New England, had important significance in secular life. The Saint James Scallop, *Pecten jacobeus* L., became a Christian religious symbol, and so has been incorporated into traditional ecclesiastical art. This happened as follows.

Saint James, disciple of Jesus, became Patron Saint of Spain. His name was attached to the Saint James Scallop as a result of an elaborate legend concerning him. It was believed that, after the Ascension of Christ, Saint James undertook the evangelization of Spain. Having little success, he returned to Jerusalem, shortly after which he was beheaded by Agrippa, as reported in the New Testament *Book of Acts*.

It is told that his disciples rescued his remains and placed them on a ship which was miraculously guided back to Spain, arriving there, according to legend, only a day after it set out from Jerusalem. According to another legend, the miraculous ship was made of marble. When it entered the harbor, a mounted knight watching on the

6. Saint James Scallop (*Pecten jacobeus* L.).

shore was thrown into the sea by his terrified horse. The knight saved himself by climbing aboard the marble vessel; his clothes, however, were completely covered with scallop shells. Because of this legend, representations of Saint James sometimes show him as a pilgrim dressed in a cloak covered with scallop shells. The saint's remains ultimately were interred in the Church of Santiago de Compostela, in the northwest corner of Spain. There, presumably, they rest today. (Photographs of the churches and art objects mentioned here may be found in the 1957 book, *The Scallop*, edited by Ian Cox.)

The association of the Scallop Shell with the cult of Saint James grew out of European religious life as it existed from the 9th to the 12th centuries. The custom of the religious pilgrimage arose in connection with the veneration of martyrs' graves and of Bible lands. It was furthered by the system of penances and privileges which brought about pilgrimages of expiation incurred, or dictated by the clergy. If one was not rich enough to pay for remission of one's sins, a pilgrimage to some distant shrine was an alternative means of restitution. The earlier pilgrimages to Rome were imposed for serious offenses. But once the system met with public acceptance it was often generalized and carried on for other reasons and purposes.

By the 11th century the church with which the Scallop Shell became associated, Santiago de Compostela, had become about as important as Rome as a goal of the pilgrim. In 1434, a Holy Year, 2,310 persons set sail from England for Spain. In addition, traveling on foot, there were hordes of penance or indulgence seekers, as well as devout tourists eager for miraculous cures, ordinary tramps, and merchants hoping to avoid tolls by their exhibition of religiosity.

Since all pilgrims covered at least part of the journey on foot, each carried with him some food, a purse or scrip, and a staff. They must have looked very much like the Mexican pilgrims who can be seen streaming through the center of Cuernavaca each summer on their several days' rugged journey to remote Chalma.

Pilgrims who actually reached the tomb of Saint James at Compostela naturally wished to carry away with them some souvenir as tangible evidence of their homage. The Scallop Shell filled the bill, both in size and in its miraculous associations. The pilgrim's guidebook *Liber Sancti Jacobi* tells how, in 1106, a knight of Apulia was cured of the goiter by the touch of a seashell.

As the same book mentions, at that time (about 1130), shells to be attached to pilgrims' purses or cloaks were on sale in the booths around the paved courts of the church, much as pictures of the Virgin of Guadalupe are on sale in booths around the shrine in the outskirts of Mexico City today. In any case, the Scallop Shell became the recognized badge of Saint James. Although it is also called the Crusader's Scallop, it is best known as the symbol of Saint James used in ecclesiastical art for over a thousand years.

A Scallop shell appears on the staff of Saint James in 14th-century Italian paintings. The shell may also be seen in some of the stained-glass windows of Chartres Cathedral, in France. Scallop shells encrust an early-16th-century palace at Salamanca, Spain. In the far northwest of Spain, in a little church built in 1778 at Pontvedra, is the figure of the Virgin as a pilgrim, with the brim of her hat turned up in front and a golden scallop shell decorating its center.

In the days before the general populace could read, such objects as the Scallop Shell were used as a means of teaching moral values. Thus it was taught that the two halves of the shell stood for the two great Commandments— Love God and Love your neighbor. The ribs symbolized the fingers of the hand, ready to perform acts of goodness and blessing.

Oddly enough, the actual species of scallop used in this way, and carried off from Compostela by the pilgrims, was not really the Saint James Scallop. Since Compostela is not on the coast, any scallops brought in for sale had to be caught by fishermen and carried inland for commercial purposes. Furthermore, communication was faulty in the days when the naturalist Linnaeus gave the name *Pecten jacobeus* to a scallop which actually comes from the other coast of Spain, and from the coasts of Italy and Sicily. But while the name *Pecten jacobeus* applies only to the one exact species, it is the Scallop Shell in a more general sense which finds its way in art and architecture as the badge of Saint James. Such matters would have bothered the pilgrims not at all. Doubtless, to such, a shell is a shell, is a shell!

7. THE EMPEROR'S TOP: SHELLS SAVE A LIFE

There is a remarkable story about two famous seashells, the Emperor's Top, *Perotrochus hirasei* Kuroda, and the Wonder Shell, *Thatcheria mirabilis* Angas. The Emperor's Top has a distinctive appearance. Austere, yet delicate, it is sumptuous both in size and in its reddish brown markings on a cream-colored background. The unusual slit near the base is unique and curious. This shell is from deep Japanese waters, and was once so rare that it commanded a price of over a hundred dollars. Today it is still a rarity, and a specimen of good color, with slit margins intact, seems to creep up nearer the hundred-dollar mark each year, and even at that is not always available. It will make one of the central pieces in any display of shells in which it is included.

The other shell, the Wonder Shell, is also fairly large, being about four inches from tip to spire. Few seashells command as much interest and admiration as this one. The spire looks like a superbly molded ramp, ascending its heights. The body swings in a winglike whorl, thin and delicate, and its flaring form and milk-white interior lend an air of refinement which reminds us of a fine porcelain teacup. A medium-sized specimen is generally to be had for about five dollars.

7. Emperor's Top (*Perotrochus hirasei* Kuroda).

An incident of World War II relating to these two shells teaches us that shell collectors are an international brotherhood. Dr. William Clench, of Harvard University, distinguished authority on shells, assures me that the story is true and agrees that these shells actually saved the life of the late noted shell collector Pedro de Mesa, with whom I frequently corresponded in the late 1950's. After the war de Mesa presented the actual specimens concerned to Dr. Clench, and they are now in the collection of the Museum of Comparative Zoology.

The story runs as follows. Some years ago, when Sr. de Mesa was a young schoolteacher, he exchanged shells with the now world-famous Japanese scientist, Tokubei Kuroda, D.Sc., the man whose name is linked with such well-known shells as *Murex pliciferoides* and *Pecten nipponensis*. It happened that Professor Kuroda's father was the general in command when the Japanese invaded the Philippines.

Among the people of Manila who fled into the mountains was de Mesa. Word reached him, however, that Professor Kuroda was in Manila, and was searching for him. Much alarmed, de Mesa sent his brother-in-law in to Manila to make inquiries.

It turned out that the purpose of the search was to make a friendly offer of a job, which de Mesa refused. He was surprised, therefore, when he received Professor Kuroda's calling-card, together with two magnificent seashells, an Emperor's Top and a Wonder Shell. When Japanese patrols finally reached de Mesa's hideout, the gift card and the two shells from Kuroda actually saved de Mesa's life.

8. THE WONDER SHELL

Some of the most remarkable seashells come from Japan. One of these is the much coveted *Thatcheria mirabilis* Angas, mentioned in the previous chapter. It was so little known a hundred years ago that one of the world's great scientists at that time thought that it was merely a freak of nature. Today it is still on the scarce side, perhaps because everyone admires and wants it. A glance at plate 8 will indicate why this shell awakens so much enthusiasm.

Even the name of this favorite shell is somewhat picturesque. Its generic name, *Thatcheria*, obviously comes from the person for whom it was named, Charles Thatcher, who brought it from Japan about 1877. Those who name shells have a way of honoring their friends, often with grotesque results in terms of verbiage, by turning the friend's name into Latin and applying it to a group of shells or to a particular species. Two collectors with whom I have corresponded in recent years have had their names attached to newly named shells. *Cypraea raysummersi* was named by a malacologist, a Professor Schilder, for a currently active West Coast collector, Ray Summers, presumably because Summers recognized the shell as an unnamed species, and sent it to Schilder for study. As I remember it, a Dr. Berry of California visited Xavier Mendoza, a Guaymas, Mexico shrimp-fleet cap-

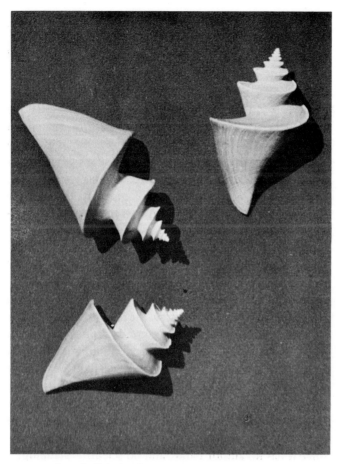

8. Wonder Shell (*Thatcheria mirabilis* Angas).

tain, who gave him an unnamed species of *Cantharus*. The shell now has the name *Cantharus mendozana* Berry.

Although the publicity value of having a shell named for one might seem like that attained by having one's name in the telephone book, actually it is something different from that. Unless it is later discovered that the shell has been named and written up by someone else at an earlier date, the name sticks as given. So the person has attained a tiny niche in the hall of fame by having his name projected into the future for unknown centuries. The name *Thatcheria mirabilis* was given to the shell by the Australian George French Angas in 1877, and probably will be used a thousand years from now.

In contrast to the relative permanence of such a scientific name as *Thatcheria mirabilis* is the transitoriness, and lack of sure standing, of such a common name as the Wonder Shell. When my wife and I first secured a photograph of it, I found that the shell seemed to have no generally used common name. The Latin word *mirabilis* means "wonderful." Combining this with my personal admiration for this shell, I decided to call it the Wonder Shell. Although this name has been frequently published as the common name of this shell, it can be displaced by anyone who writes a book, or who prefers some other name. Since it is English, it is not international. Since it has no author name, and no scientific standing, it may disappear tomorrow.

The shell itself, however, has persisted and will probably persist through unknown millenniums. It is an amazing combination of fragility and beauty. Since such delicacy and beauty are dominant aspects of classical

Japanese art, one might dream that this shell had been designed by some great Japanese sculptor. Its outer form is elegant and refined. Beginning at the tip of a pointed spiral, it slips down gracefully to the body whorl in a smooth ramp. The largest whorl swings wide and, making up the largest portion of the shell, is astonishingly graceful. Outside, the color is light tan to pinkish.

Since the Wonder Shell grows in deep water at about eighty to a hundred fathoms, it is not secured without great human effort. Breakage is common, so that imperfect specimens are filed back. But even so they retain most of their beauty. The best, smooth, unfiled shells, of good color, and without growth flaws, are especially scarce, and worth more than average good specimens.

The American malacologist who, about two decades less than a hundred years ago, was puzzled by this shell was none less than the famed George W. Tryon, of the Academy of Natural Sciences of Philadelphia. He wrote in his *Manual of Conchology: Structural and Systematic* (Tryon, G. W., and Pilsbry, H. A.: Academy of Sciences, Philadelphia, 1879–1935; out of print) as follows: "That this shell is a scaliform monstrosity cannot be doubted, but what may be its normal form is not so readily ascertained. I saw the single specimen . . . in London, in 1887, and was immediately convinced that the conical form, flattened shoulders, and sinus were all due to distorted growth." Probably the very specimen seen by Tryon was the shell brought from Japan by Mr. Thatcher, said to be the largest ever found. It is in Mrs. de Burgh's collection in the British Museum. No others were known until the 1930's, when others were brought from Japan.

9. DEBUT OF
THE GIANT CLAM

From time immemorial the Giant Clam has lived as a huge denizen of the deeps off the Philippines and Australia. Only recently, however, did this magnificent shell make its bow as the center of a celebration in the United States. At that time a 300-pound shell was presented, in a special ceremony held on a Circle Line ship in New York harbor, to the Circumnavigator's Club. The stunning gift was made by the Australian Travel Association. This particular shell is said to be the largest ever displayed here, but I have seen others probably as large, like the huge specimen outdoors along the walk at Mystic Seaport, Connecticut.

The Giant Clam, *Tridacna gigas* L., is the world's largest mollusk, land or sea, bivalve or univalve. There is a record of a shell from Sumatra which weighs 507 pounds. Very close to it is probably the largest specimen ever exhibited, which is to be seen in the Australian Museum at Sydney; its weight is 500 pounds. It measures just over three feet along the valve. A twelve-month-old baby, protected by well-padded woolen clothes, has slept comfortably in this very shell.

The Giant Clam is widely distributed and has a remarkable life pattern. It is found throughout the South

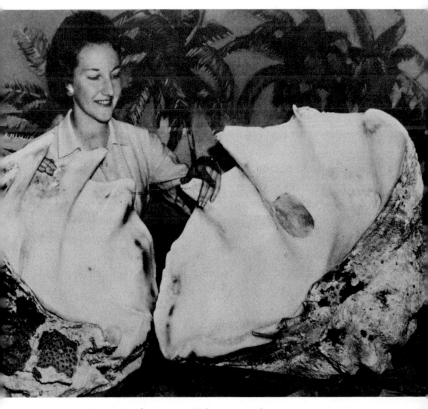

9. Giant Clam (*Tridacna gigas* L.).
Photograph courtesy of Cunningham and Walsh, Inc., New York, N.Y.

Pacific, and in abundance along the northern half of the 12,500-mile Great Barrier Reef, off the eastern coast of Australia. The early traveler, Captain Cook, recorded its presence here as "cockles of so enormous a size that one of them was more than two men could eat." They are still eaten today.

Seen live, in its own natural setting, the Giant Clam is an astonishing spectacle. Sometimes it is found wedged between boulders, or covered with so much overgrowth that it is hardly distinguishable. Usually it simply lies flat on the bottom, valves slightly gaping, so that the olive-green or brown mantle is brilliantly colored peacock blue, pink, green, or red-brown.

Its "eyes" are a phenomenon in themselves. They appear as bright emerald spots but are not true eyes. They are conical structures called "hyaline organs" used to pipe light into the interior of the clam. The light helps support a species of alga that grows inside the body of the clam, which acts as its host. This symbiotic phenomenon was identified by Dr. C. M. Yonge during the British Expedition of 1928–29. He found the unicellular algae, called *zoozanthellae,* living in association or partnership with the clam.

These algae were found in clusters about the hyaline organs, and traced on through the digestive system of the clam, which first farms them, and then devours them. Perhaps this amazing process of raising part of their own food, within their own mantle, may explain why these clams never have to go hungry, and thus have been able to support their immense size.

The word *clam* has such wide significance that it merely

means a bivalve. What we call clams in the United States, however, are small edible creatures, such as the Soft-shelled Clam, *Mya arenaria* L., eaten as delicacies on both our eastern and western coasts. The clams of the Australians are rather those very different-appearing shells called *Tridacna,* among which is the Frilled Clam.

Dr. Iredale, of Australia, has maintained that the name is properly not *Tridacna gigas* L., but preferably *Tridacna derasa* Bolten. But the *gigas,* meaning "giant," seems to stick.

Moving pictures and tall tales of divers caught between the valves of a Giant Clam, to make their escape with, or without, an arm or a leg may be discounted, probably 100 per cent. The quiescent clam is hardly a voracious, marauding creature, but a calm consumer of a mild diet of home-prepared algae.

10. ONCE A MYSTERY: THE PAPER NAUTILUS

The Paper Nautilus, or Argonaut, is an odd mollusk because its shell is an egg cradle, and not a skeletal support to its soft parts. It would save some confusion if we used for it only the secondary common name Argonaut, following the Latin name *Argonauta*. This would avoid the mixup with the Chambered Nautilus, another favorite of collectors, which gets its common name from its entirely different generic name, the Latin *Nautilus*.

To differentiate, the Argonaut is a free-swimming octopus. It is not attached to its shell, the latter being no part of its skeletal structure. The Chambered Nautilus, on the other hand, is attached to its shell, as is the case with most of the hundreds of thousands of other mollusks in that huge phylum. The shell is, in a sense, a very part of it. But in spite of this considerable difference, for about two thousand years, from the time Aristotle described them until the middle of the last century, the two shells have been confused with one another.

This confusion has been projected into the indefinite future by Oliver Wendell Holmes, who mixed up the supposed characteristics of the two very different creatures in his famous poem "The Chambered Nautilus." The Chambered Nautilus is sturdy, and not uncommon

10. Paper Nautilus.

in its native Pacific seas. Its habits are still a bit of a mystery. The Argonaut, or Paper Nautilus, on the other hand, is very fragile and very scarce.

What, then, have the two species in common so that both are named Nautilus? They both live in warm tropical waters and they resemble one another in general size and shape. That's about all.

The life and ways of the Paper Nautilus are now no mystery. They can be read in complete detail in an article by Roy Waldo Miner in *National Geographic Magazine* (August, 1935). For a long time, however, it had been a subject of contradiction and controversy. About the middle of the last century, as modern science began to awaken interest in nature, new attention began to be paid to this odd, plastic-like, paper-thin "boat," which was found floating in warm seas and was inhabited by a "now-you-have-it-now-you-don't" sort of creature. At that time Mrs. Jeanette Power, a French lady living in Sicily, watched the Argonaut in a tank. She also sent specimens to be studied by scientists in the capitals of Europe.

Up to then some naturalists had held odd views about the Argonaut. They believed that, just as the cuckoo borrows a nest, and lays its eggs there for another bird to hatch, so an octopus left eggs to be hatched by the strange creature found sitting in the Paper Nautilus shell, clutching the shell by means of two flattened-out arms extended and spread out over the exterior sides of the cradle. Its eyes peeped out over the opening, and waves of color swept over it as it moved in breathing.

In the end it was found out that the flexible shell was excreted by the two arms spread out over the outside.

The Cowry, similarly, deposits lime to make its shell by spreading a soft fleshy mantle from its opening all over its outer parts.

The full story is a strange one. The Argonaut is an octopus. The Octopus is known as a Cephalopod, a name derived from the Greek words for "head" and "foot." When it swims the bulbous hump moves forward, the arms streaming behind. When it crawls on the bottom the hump is up, so the head and mouth are down, and the Octopus, as it were, stands on its head.

Male and female, these little creatures disport in warm seas. At breeding time the male Argonaut approaches the female and drops the male copulatory organ, laden with spermatozoa, into the female's mantle cavity. There the organ remains for a certain time, fertilizing the eggs so that they hatch at last and the babies are set free.

Several varieties of the Paper Nautilus may be found anywhere in warm seas. But the *Argonauta argo* L. tends to be found off the eastern United States, and the *Argonauta nodosa* Solander off Australia. They look much alike, both being large, with translucent white shells trimmed neatly with brownish black.

Beautiful white Paper Nautilus shells are expensive, priced in America at about eight dollars for a five-inch specimen, twelve dollars for a six-inch shell, and twenty-five dollars for an eight-inch one. There is a smaller brownish shell, *Argonauta hians* Solander, about two inches in length, which is more common.

No wonder the Paper Nautilus is much wanted. In both its appearance and its life story it is a marvel of nature.

11. THE ELUSIVE
MUSIC VOLUTE

One does not expect to find the musical score for a folk song written by nature on the surface of a seashell, nor does one find any such thing. But, surprisingly enough, there is one Caribbean shell which may be marked so distinctly with the lines and notes of what looks like a musical staff that it is called the Music Volute (*Voluta musica* Sowerby).

Some shells, like the scarce *Voluta aulica* Sowerby of the Philippines, are obtainable on order, but only after a wait of four months. The Music Volute, however, is in spasmodic supply. It may be available at some times, and virtually unobtainable at others. This I personally ascribe to the temperament of some of the natives of the Caribbean area. The character of Americans is generally such that a business order is a command, and it must be met, whatever the cost to one's nervous system. In the Caribbean area, and in some countries south of the United States, the rhythm of life seems to be different.

An American visiting Mexico took a great fancy to the work of a certain potter in Oaxaca. He priced an article and then asked for a hundred of them. But the potter raised the price per article if that quantity were to be made. In other words, he refused the order. To make a

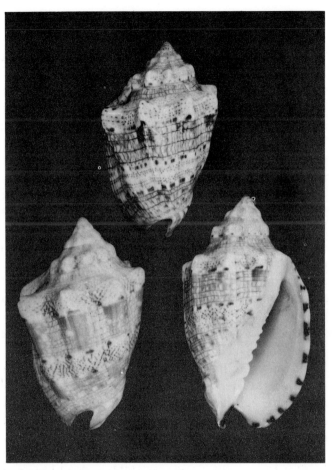

11. Music Volute (*Voluta musica* Sowerby).

few would keep life in balance, but a large order would cause unnecessary enslavement.

Some years ago the widow of the naturalist-author Hyatt Verrill gave me the name of a native of Trinidad from whom a resident there had obtained fine specimens of the Music Volute. I wrote repeatedly, requesting shells, but got no answer. Five years later another resident of Trinidad sent me some beauties. He had obtained them from the same fisherman who had ignored my written requests.

Occasionally it is possible to get these shells from the waters off Margarita Island, Venezuela. These are the largest and most shapely that I have seen. Unfortunately, up to now, I have been unable to secure any of them direct. A smaller, less shapely variety, not so well marked, comes from the vicinity of Martinique, in the West Indies. These are sometimes available and I get what I can, when I can.

Phenomena like the odd appearance of "music" on the Music Volute tend to make a shell popular and wanted. For example, something like Hebrew writing or characters on the Hebrew Volute, *Volute ebraea* L., a shell whose size and shape make it a companion piece of the Music Volute, has the effect of prodding collectors into ownership.

Some years ago Satis N. Coleman, the author of the best book on teaching music to children that I have ever seen (*Creative Music for Children,* G. P. Putnam's Sons: New York, 1922) was a teacher of music in the then Lincoln School of Columbia University, in New York City. She accomplished most unusual results with the children in her classes. Some of the brighter pupils learned to take any three notes and, with help, build them into a symphony. Perhaps, some day, notes that appear on a specimen of the Music Volute will inspire a musician to write a Seashell Symphony.

12. A COSMETIC SHELL

It seems one never ceases to come across different uses for seashells. They are used as charms, as properties in moving pictures, as personal and home decorations, and for centuries they were used for money. A use new to me turned up while I was in Puerto Marques, Mexico, near Acapulco, the site of one of the most perfect bays for swimming and light sailing in the world. Protected from the fury of the ocean waves on nearby beaches, like Revolcadero, it can be entered only by a very narrow inlet. Every day of the year, local inhabitants and tourists who want something that is cleaner and less crowded than the in-town beaches come to relax in the sun and spend hours in and out of the incredibly comfortable water of the bay.

Puerto Marques may be reached by car, bus, or boat from Acapulco in half an hour. I often buy shells there from a fisherman who lives in a thatched beach pavilion called Pez Vela, "The Sailfish." Each year I seek him out and spend some hours at a table, usually in my bathing suit, after a good swim. I sit under his thatched roof with a cool drink, while my host brings out shells from shelves and buckets and lays them out in little piles for my inspection and selection.

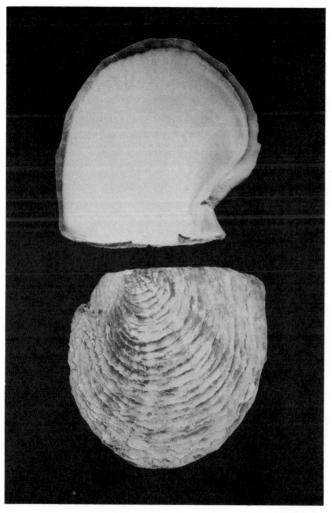

12. West Mexico Pearl Oyster (*Pinctada mazatlanica* Hanley).

Many of the shells have blemishes or defects and I have to choose slowly and carefully. After an hour of by-play I start to bargain. I offer so much for each shell, sum it up on paper, and then, at the "hesitation-point," add a little more to the total to smooth out the deal in good trading fashion. The whole process is a form of entertainment for us both, a drama in which we enjoy taking part.*

On my last visit I was amazed to find that my host did not want to accept my price for a rather ordinary pearl shell usually worth very little. So I pursued the conversation to see if I could find out why. It was simple. This particular shell, *Pinctada mazatlanica* Hanley, brought him a higher price elsewhere, because it was in demand by those who know how to make from it a cosmetic preparation which is useful to cover and hide facial blemishes, or scars that remain after lacerations or operations.

By chance, a friend of mine in Cuernavaca told me that he had paid quite a price for one of these shells in Mexico City for use by his wife, who had a temporary scar on her face. When I asked the lady how the preparation was made she gave me the following directions. I see no reason why anyone owning a pearl shell should not try them.

The bivalve, which the Mexicans call Concha de Nacre, must be somewhat arduously scraped to free the nacre into a powder that is slowly collected in the basin of the shell. Over this is squeezed the juice of a lime and the whole is mixed into a small pool in the shell. This is then put in a cool place and allowed to stand overnight. When

* On later visits I found Pez Vela had a new name. The little restaurants remain, but none any longer sell seashells.

the resulting paste seems to be of the right consistency it may be applied to cover the blemish. The result is said to be quite satisfactory.

This process has been commercialized in Mexico City, and a cosmetic made from this shell may be bought in some of the downtown luxury shops. The powder is mixed, I believe, with lanolin, into a cream called Crema de Nacre. What other shells may be used in a similar way to exploit this beauty secret I do not know. This might make an interesting experiment for anyone inclined to try it.

13. A "PRECIOUS" SEASHELL

One of the most admired and cherished of all small shells is called by the odd name of Precious Wentletrap. It is so well known that its picture may be found in illustrated editions of Webster's dictionary. Under the word *wentletrap* the dictionary reports that the derivation is from the German *wendeltreppe*, "a spiral staircase."

The name Wentletrap is given not only to this shell, but to a number of others of similar shape scattered in the waters of the world's oceans. Each shell of this group is called, in scientific language, an *Epitonium*. The Precious Wentletrap itself is a glistening white, with a finish that makes it look as if it were fashioned of the finest porcelain, delicately shaped. It is the kind of shell that collectors like to put in a nest of white or blue cotton wool, because it is like a jewel, or a work of art.

It is no ordinary shell, picked up accidentally at the seaside. It comes from deep water in an area from the China Sea to Northern Australia, and is usually dredged or brought up by divers or by a hurricane. By no means is it a discovery of modern shell collectors, for it has been valued and sought for generations. About the year 1770 shells from the China Sea brought a price as high as $200, and it was counterfeited by Chinese artisans in rice flour. No wonder it is called Precious.

13. Precious Wentletrap (*Epitonium scalare* L.).

Today the shell is not too easy to secure in fine condition, but is not so rare as to be beyond the reach of the average collector. Shells ranging in size from $1\frac{1}{2}$ to 2 inches sell for about four to eight dollars each, when obtainable.

The shell is admired for its delicate curves formed as a remarkable series of whorls, continuous yet almost separate. Its spiral form has been an inspiration to architects as the natural prototype of the spiral staircase.

The scientific name of this shell has undergone several changes which make it hard to locate in shell books. In some it is listed as *Epitonium pretiosum* Lam., in others as *Scala scalare* L. But in some recent books it is *Epitonium scalare* L. Here then is an interesting and unusual case in which a common name has remained more permanent than the scientific one, an exception, we hope, which does not disprove the contention that scientific names are best.

In any case the wentletraps, of which quite a number are available, make an excellent group for collectors who want to get a group of related shells of a single genus. Except for the largest of them, *Epitonium magnificum* Sowerby, from Japan, which can reach a length of $4\frac{1}{4}$ inches (and a few others), they are not expensive. In fact, in many areas a local species can usually be collected.

Our New England pride and joy is a tiny white species to be found on Cape Cod. Often when I have gone to the monthly meeting of the Boston Malacological Club at Harvard I have had a few words with Dr. Merrill E. Champion (now deceased), a physician who was a shell expert in this field for years. The tiny Cape Cod wentletrap is named *Epitonium championi* Clench after him.

A collector who begins with a wentletrap from his own locality can gradually add such attractive small specimens as *Epitonium stigmaticum*, which has dark red spots, and *Epitonium pallasi*, which resembles a small specimen of the Precious Wentletrap. There are some taller, more turreted species, such as *Epitonium kurohari*, another rarity. Gradually it is possible to get together a beautiful collection of this genus. Such a collection is sure to evoke admiration.

14. THE EMERALD SNAIL

A shiny land shell, the Emerald Snail, is of such sharp color, and of such a sylvan green, it is coveted by many collectors. Like many popular shells, *Papuina pulcherrima* is the more valued because the facts and stories about it are intrinsically interesting.

A decade ago it was rated in the United States as rare. The late Dr. Erasmus Alsaker, a prominent shell collector, at that time bought one of these green beauties for ten dollars. With it he won an award in a Florida shell show. If my memory serves me correctly, his *Papuina pulcherrima* was designated "Shell of the Show," and everyone concerned seemed pleased in the matter.

The scarcity of the shell, at that time, was due to the fact it was found only on Manus, one of the Admiralty Islands, a place once so difficult of access that few of the shells ever left the Island. It was reported that, in earlier days, some shells were brought across to the mainland in canoes. But this seems an unlikely story.

A few days after I learned of Dr. Alsaker's award I received a startling letter by air from Manus. To my astonishment a resident of the island offered to send me all the emerald snails I wanted for a sum so nominal I laughed aloud.

14. Emerald Snail (*Papuina pulcherrima* Rensch).

It seems these snails, although they live only in one forest area of the world, nevertheless lurk in their own jungle habitat in large numbers. When I learned this I recalled a remark made by Harvard's famed malacologist, Dr. William Clench, that he once saw "a bucketful" of them.

Their abundance on location does not mean that gathering them is easy. If a farmer clears away a bit of vegetation, however, the snails lose their immediate habitat and are readily picked up from the ground and nearby plants.

It seems that children sent to hunt them can usually find specimens. Sometimes the snails are put on sale in the local market, presumably as food.

My friend, when he gathered his first lot, put them in a pail of water for a day or so but was disturbed to find that the water had become polluted and had destroyed the shells' shiny finish. A new lot had to be collected.

Actually, even with the best lots, there is a wide variance in quality from shell to shell. Many must be discarded. A good shell may have spots, or be duller than others, while the large, shiny, unblemished green shells are quite scarce in any lot, and so are worth considerably more.

The Emerald Snail, *Papuina pulcherrima* Rensch, was first collected in quantity by the Whitney South Seas Expedition in 1933. The species had been described a short time earlier by Ilsa Rensch from a specimen collected by a Father Schneider.

The habitat of *Papuina pulcherrima* is twenty or more feet above the ground in jungle trees. The snails probably feed at night on lichens and fungal films on the bark of the trees, then by day seek shelter from the heat and light by hiding under the large leaves of a creeper that grows around many of the trees. The snails also are found in Sago palms in swampy sections or beside streams, and for that reason are called Sac-Sac Snails. Sac-Sac is a native name for Sago.

A beautiful colored card has been made as a print from a painting showing four of the live snails set against green jungle background. I have one of these cards, sent me from Manus, but I cannot be sure how they may be obtained. Anyone interested might inquire of the artist, Captain Brett Hilder, 183 Edinburgh Road, Castlecrag, N. S. W., Australia. His name appears under the printed description of the lovely *Papuina pulcherrima*.

15. THE GOLDEN COWRY

Top glamour shell of all shells is probably the Golden Cowry. It has about all the features that make a shell a conversation piece. In the first place it has an ideal size, varying around three inches. This makes it large enough to be noticeable, but not too large for the cramped space of a collection. Its color, close to orange-pink, is bright enough to permit it the opulent name Golden.

Not only is it rare, but it has an aristocratic history. In tribal times the chiefs of the Fiji Islands wore pierced Golden Cowry shells about their necks as a sign of royalty.

The shell is actively sought by divers in seas stretching from Fiji to the Philippines. It seems to thrive only in warm waters. Specimens have been reported from the Loyalty Islands, Yap, in the Caroline Islands, and the Marshall Islands; from Nadroga Reef, south of Viti Levu, in the Fiji Islands; and from Surigao and Davao on the eastern shores of Mindanao in the Philippines.

A few have been discovered as far north as the Mariannas, and as far east as the Society Islands and the Tuamotu Archipelago. Previously natives may have kept secret the place where shells were found, but recently it has been established that the Golden Cowry lives in fairly shallow water on ledges of coral.

On a search promoted by the request of the distin-

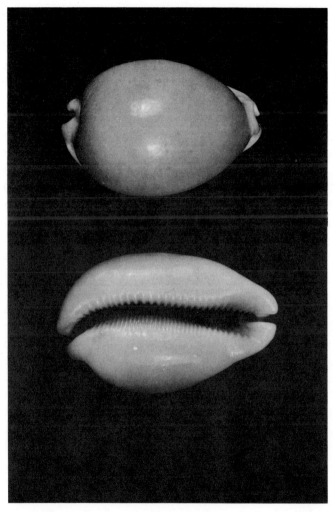

15. Golden Cowry (*Callistocypraea aurantium aurantium* Gmelin).

guished collector Karl W. Green, of Hawaii, in 1962, a Mr. Lahora, of Maray, in the Philippines, and his godson made a number of unsuccessful night trips. But, at last, on June 12 at 11 P.M., they caught a specimen. Apparently it had taken its evening meal and gone to bed in a little cave in the coral.

This kind of habitat seems to be typical, for a diver who found one in 1960, outside a barrier reef in French Polynesia, reported that his specimen was found in about twenty feet of water, hidden in a narrow crevice. This Tahitian had to dive fifteen times before he could pinch the shell between the bars of his spear. There is good reason to prize a shell so difficult to discover and to catch.

The price of this superb shell goes up, and occasionally down. But since the demand has exceeded the supply in recent years, it seems to have become more and more costly. Less than a decade ago a fair specimen could sometimes be had for fifty dollars. In 1949, my wife's father, Alden Strong, had a letter from Hyatt Verrill, the author, saying he had been offered six specimens from Australia, but had not been tempted enough to buy them. He had sold his "last super," he wrote, for forty dollars.

Even today a knowledgeable person might pick up a bargain; in 1962, a collector bought a fair specimen in a Cape Cod shop for only fifty cents. On the other hand, several years ago a wealthy lady, traveling in Fiji, paid $250 for one, on the spot.

The best offer I have had in several years for a fresh-caught Golden Cowry came from a reliable acquaintance in Fiji who promised to get me one for $150. Since he asked for the money in advance, the risk was too great.

It is a fairly safe rule never to send money in advance to a foreign country for shells, since too many hazards are involved. In one case a well-known dealer, in the Orient, from whom we had received shells for years, asked for money in advance, got it, then defaulted. We have never heard from him since. There is no recourse, in such cases, for the collector who has sent money to a foreign dealer.

Every year many pages are written and many new stories told about the Golden Cowry. One of the recent tales comes from a sophisticated collector who was traveling on a Pacific steamship when he learned of an oiler who had gotten hold of a specimen. By the time the collector reached the engine room to make a bid for the shell he found that its owner had sliced off the top and turned the shell into a pen-holder.

The Golden Cowry, *Callistocypraea aurantium aurantium* Gmelin, continues to hold its place of distinction, with no diminution in the struggle for a good specimen. Actually it is something of a status symbol, signifying that the collector-owner is wise, has money to spare, and is to be reckoned with as an important collector. Anyone who has a Golden Cowry is "one-up" on those poor souls who are only aspiring.

So distinguished are the owners of a Golden Cowry that they may register their shell, with its dimensions, in the Golden Cowry Register kept by the Hawaiian Shell Club. Since the institution of this register, the popularity and the price of this shell of shells have gone up rapidly.

The Golden Cowry has its own peculiar distinction and good looks which will always enable it to consort with wealth and royalty.

SPECIAL GROUPS
OF SHELLS

16. THE FASCINATING CONE SHELLS

The cone shells, of the genus *Conus*, form one of the most popular groups of shells. A. F. Marsh quotes the famed conchologist John Mawe who, writing about 1835, said: "There is, perhaps, no other genus which holds so important a station in collections as *Conus*, a distinction to which it is entitled from the matchless beauty and endless variety of the species."

As short a time as ten years ago great confusion existed among some of the species of cone shells. Their identification was most difficult. Recently, however, collectors have been much encouraged toward beginning a collection of cones because much new illustrated material has come to our aid.

Cone shells get their name from the simple fact that they are cone-shaped. Their delightful variations are due, in part, to a large variety of markings. Cones can be almost plain in a flat color, like the yellowish *Conus virgo;* or tented, like the fancy *Conus textile;* or banded like *Conus miles;* or dotted, splotched, or mottled, like several other species.

Furthermore, cones come in many colors. Some are spotted with bright red, like *Conus tessulatus;* or touched with blue, like some specimens of *Conus praelatus;* or

16. Species of *Conus* Shells. ROW 1, FROM LEFT: *Conus betulinus* L.; *C. geographus* L.; *C. virgo* L.; *C. leopardus* Röding. ROW 2: *C. marmoreus* L.; *C. marmoreus bandanus* Hwass; *C. namocanus* Hwass; *C. vexillum* Gmelin; *C. litteratus* L. ROW 3: *C. striatus* L.; *C. distans* Hwass; *C. textile* L.; *C. nicobaricus* Hwass; *C. nicobaricus* Hwass. ROW 4: *C. aulicus* L.; *C. aulicus* L.; *C. quercinus* Lightfoot; *C. imperialis* L.; *C. fergusoni* Sowerby.

tinged with violet, like *Conus ione.* Not only are there wide variations in marking and coloration, but there is some differentiation in shape. While all are generally cone-shaped, there are cones which are thin and sleek, like *Conus orbignyi;* chubby cones, like *Conus betulinus;* cones with flat tops, like *Conus litteratus;* and others with a high pointed spire, like *Conus generalis.*

Most cones that appear in collections are from $1\frac{1}{2}$ to 2 inches tip to tip. But there are tiny cones, like *Conus rutilus,* $\frac{1}{2}$ inch long. A very large species, *Conus prometheus,* can measure as much as 6 inches.

Many cones are relatively plentiful in their native seas and so are priced around a dollar, like *Conus striatellus.* Others, such as *Conus gloriamaris,* are scarce and rare.

Cones in all their remarkable variety and beauty can now be seen arranged in color pictures in a book only recently available, *Cone Shells of the World* (1964). It is by two Australians, the writer Dr. A. F. Marsh and the artist O. H. Rippingale. In it, nearly 500 species are drawn in color (not photographed). This book is a monumental piece of work. It provides collectors of cone shells with the essential guidance they have hitherto been without. Merely as a picture book, this volume is superb. It should be a delight to many who are not collectors at all but are fascinated by a book on cones, just as they would be by a color book on butterflies.

As I look at the pictures it seems to me that, at times, the artist has seen more color in some of the cones than is likely to be found in most individuals of the species. Perhaps especially colorful examples were chosen for portrayal. As a result, some collectors may be baffled in an attempt to secure specimens as colorful as those shown. In any set of ten cones of a given species, there will probably be eight or nine with less color than the brightest one. Cones in high color tend to be scarce, and so more costly.

The book is an additional pleasure to use because Dr. Marsh has solved a problem of presentation never previously solved by any of the writers of notable shell books. He has met the demands of both scientists and non-scientific collectors, devising a clever plan by which the shells are shown in related groups under a heading. For a long time collectors have been bothered by the use of sub-generic names like *Rhizoconus* and *Lithoconus,* names which might be regarded as works of supererogation. Dr. Marsh has used these group names only at the top of a group, listing all cones by their convenient generic name of *Conus,* below these group names. Thus we find the familiar names of *Conus victoriae, Conus princeps,* and *Conus omaria.* Those who wish may label their shells so, or may write in the sub-generic names on their own labels. This is comforting, since there is something basically right about calling a cone a cone.

17. POISON CONES

The animals in most seashells are harmless. Recently, however, a collector named Ronald Pahl had a most unpleasant experience on a shell-gathering trip out from Fiji. The *Hawaiian Shell News* tells the story somewhat as follows.

Ronald is on the staff of Fulton College, Tailevu, Fiji. He is an excellent diver and spear fisherman who took off on a collecting trip to Samoa. He was searching there on a reef, about a mile from shore at Apia, when he discovered a group of seven specimens of the Tulip Cone, *Conus tulipa* L. It was hard to hold so many specimens at once, so he let some of them lie still on his hand while he gathered the others. As one of them began to slip off, he flicked it with his finger and the cone suddenly either bit or stung him. In a few minutes his hand was numb.

He used a tourniquet made from the strap of his diving mask. The numbness, however, continued to spread. Knowing the danger, he got to a doctor as quickly as possible, but not before the numbness had spread to his whole arm, and across his chest. The doctor injected an antihistamine in one arm and adrenalin in the other. The chest constriction vanished immediately, but it was two days before he could move his little and third fingers. Ten

17. Poison Cones. ROW I, FROM LEFT: Marble Cone (*Conus marmoreus* L.); Geographer's Cone (*C. geographus* L.); Striated Cone (*C. striatus* L.). ROW 2: Courtly Cone (*Conus aulicus* L.); Tulip Cone (*C. tulipa* L.); Textile Cone (*C. textile* L.).

days later his hand was as numb as ever, but complete recovery was expected.

This is by no means the only account of the effects of a sting by one of the six poison cones, the most distinguished of which is the rather rare Courtly Cone, *Conus aulicus* L., shown in plate 17. The other five commonly listed are: the Tulip Cone, *Conus tulipa* L.; the Cloth-of-Gold Cone, *Conus textile* L.; the Marbled Cone, *Conus marmoreus* L.; the Striated Cone, *Conus striatus* L.; and the one regarded as the most venomous of all, *Conus geographus* L. (the Geographer Cone, so named because its markings are thought to resemble land masses on a map). All of these cones are inhabitants of the Indo-Pacific region, most of them being found on the Great Barrier Reef of Australia.

The sting of the animals that live in these cones varies in effect from nothing more serious than a bee sting, to violent reactions which in some cases result in death. No thorough or complete study of the subject has yet been made by scientists, nor is there any complete account of the whole matter anywhere in print.

Cone stings have been reported for centuries but, considering the thousands of cone shells collected, remarkably few casualties and very few deaths have been reported. One of the more recent was that of Theophile Gnai, of Pouebo in New Caledonia, who on 5 November, 1960, while diving, was stung in the middle of the hand by a *Conus geographus* which he had just caught. The pain was so severe he was rushed to the local dispensary, where the nurse took charge, but all too late. He died within two hours after he had been bitten.

The mechanism of the sting is described as a narrow tooth, like a hollow barbed needle, that grows at the end of the mollusk's "snout" or proboscis. Cones are shy creatures who of course do not "attack" man. They live by boring into the shells of other mollusks, then sucking out the juices. Cones live in crevices and hollows in rocks and reefs. They retract when caught, and lie quiet. The danger arises only when they are left to stand, as the fleshy parts begin to creep out. The poison from a gland is shot out, much as a snake projects venom, and the sharp tooth can pierce the soft human skin. The tooth is called a *radula*.

Except for *Conus aulicus*, these shells are not rare, and all are handsome. A collection of the shells of these six best-known poison mollusks, with proper descriptions and notes, would make an excellent exhibit for a Science Fair. Although my wife has unusually fine and large specimens of each of them in her collection, I have yet to see them grouped together, much less photographed together in one picture.

American collectors are glad to know that no cones found in waters of the American coasts are poisonous. If there is any danger in collecting shells from these coasts it is not from the mollusks themselves.

18. THE CARRIERS

Because it carries other shells on what might be called its back, the Carrier Shell, sometimes named the Collector Shell, is a continuing topic of conversation among shell collectors. Most carrier shells are of the genus *Xenophora* (Carrier of a Stranger). They are widely scattered over the globe, in tropical waters.

Only a few weeks ago I received my first specimens of the largest of them all, the Giant Carrier Shell, *Xenophora gigantea* Schepman, from Japan. It is a thinnish shell in the characteristic toplike shape, and has few attachments. To my surprise I saw that one of the specimens had added tiny dead Tusk Shells at its outer edge, from which they stuck out like scimitars.

The shell in plate 18 is the Pale or Pallid Carrier, *Xenophora pallidula* Reeve, also from Japan. Since it was photographed from above, in order to show the agglomeration of attachments, the shell's apex at the center and its toplike shape are not visible here. But plate 18 does show the extraordinary mixture of stones, shells, and miscellaneous debris with which the creature had covered itself, and the precision of the placement.

This creature's ability to make itself look like a patch of dead shells is regarded by scientists as a protective

18. Pallid Carrier Shell (*Xenophora pallidula* Reeve).

device. It enables the mollusk to disappear from sight against a background of similar-appearing materials. But whatever the intention of creation in the matter, this odd behavior does awaken our special interest in these unusual gastropods.

Our wonder is aroused by the instinctive mechanism enabling these creatures to collect and attach to their own shells an armor or decoration of miscellaneous materials from the sea bottom. How is this small creature able to select from the surrounding environment materials suitable in size and texture for its purpose? Two of the most spectacular examples, in terms of their neat pattern of attached shells, are the Pale Carrier (see plate 18), and the Robust Carrier, *Xenophora robusta* Verrill, from the opposite side of the Pacific, on the West Coast of Mexico. They look so much alike that they could be considered the same species if it were not for the fact that the latter has a large orange-brown patch at the opening. This patch is entirely missing in its Japanese cousin.

These shells begin to grow from their apexes, at the tops of their cones. At first they fasten on small bits of dead shells, broken fragments small enough to be fastened in place, by whatever remarkable cement the tiny creatures use for their purpose. As the shell grows, a new edging or trimming of larger shells and bits is fixed on at the edge, with a downward slope. In a mature shell the last added border of shells is usually made up of single valves of bivalves, all of approximately the same size, protruding from the outer edge of the shell itself with a fascinating scalloping effect.

It is true that if you drop a handful of clam shells in the

water the shape of the valve makes them sink to the bottom with convex side uppermost. Even so, it seems unbelievable that the carrier shells can decorate themselves by attaching one after another of these half-shells completely around the outer edge, every shell turned with the same side up. In the end a well-trimmed carrier shell might look like a fancy and fascinating lady's hat.

There are several other species of carrier shells found in Japanese waters. Color photographs of these are shown in the books of Tetsuaki Kira and Tadashige Habe (see p. 327). Three species are shown in R. Tucker Abbott's large volume, *American Sea Shells* (1954), including what is probably one of the smallest of them, the two-inch Atlantic Carrier Shell, *Xenophora conchyliophora* Born. The cardboard-thin, delicate *Xenophora solaris* Reeve, a rarity, is to be seen in Walter Freeman Webb's *Handbook for Shell Collectors* (1971) and in Abbott's *Sea Shells of the World* (1962), where it is called *Stellaria solaris*. Strangely enough, this shell is not a carrier of other shells but provides its own marginal spurs.

Some years ago Mrs. Margaret Teskey, Executive Secretary of the American Malacological Union, began to make a collection of the carrier shells. Surprisingly enough, it took her quite some time to get specimens of all of them, and obtaining them was a real achievement. It would seem that a special collection is quite a satisfactory objective for a collector who wants to own specimens of all the known species of some particular genus. Not only will the collection remain a relatively small one, but it will be attractive and be something of a challenge to bring to completion.

19. THE COWRY MENAGERIE

Probably no species of shells has had such interesting names given to its members as the cowries. The flashy name Money Cowry has made that tiny yellow shell famous. There are such odd names as Sieve Cowry, Little Ass Cowry, Wood Louse Cowry and Carnelian Cowry, the latter being a shell often mistaken by amateurs for the Golden Cowry. These names, like those which follow in this section, are translations from the Latin.

One special lot of cowries we may group together for the sake of interest and call the Cowry Menagerie. With a certain flair for the picturesque, early scientists had a fancy for giving semi-descriptive names to shells, providing a slightly poetic touch. This picturesque quality remains, even in our own time, because the names persist in scientific form through the centuries. In earlier days, when the game of giving scientific names was just beginning, there were many unnamed shells, so scientists had plenty of freedom to exercise their imaginations in the naming process.

Today most shells have been discovered and named, and a scientist is more likely to give the name of a person to the new shell, thus providing that person a certain

19. Cowries. ROW 1, FROM LEFT: Little Deer (*Cypraea cervinetta* Kiener); Mole (*C. talpa* L.); Lynx (*C. lynx* L.). ROW 2: Panther (*Cypraea pantherina* Solander); Mouse (*C. mus* L.); Calf (*C. vitellus* L.).

permanence by arranging to have his name carried to posterity. An example is the case of the beautiful little cowry *Cypraea coxeni* Cox, which will carry the name of Cox into indefinite futurity.

Many of the cowries of the Cowry Menagerie were named by Linnaeus. It was he who named the most famous of all the Cowry Menagerie, the Tiger Cowry. This shell has been popular for centuries, and thousands who never owned another shell have a Tiger Cowry either on display or tucked away among their possessions. The Tiger Cowry is as much sought after today as ever. A carefully chosen series shows astonishingly rich color variations, and shells with an unusual color pattern are much prized. An acquaintance who flew in from the Marshall Islands told me that native divers there do a brisk trade in these cowries at prices sometimes higher than those the shell brings in the United States.

What might be called the wild-animal group includes:
The Tiger Cowry, *Cypraea tigris* L., Indo-Pacific;
The Panther Cowry, *Cypraea pantherina* Solander, Red Sea;
The Little Bear Cowry, *Cypraea ursellus* Gmelin, Indo-Pacific;
The Lynx Cowry, *Cypraea lynx* L., Indo-Pacific.

These are the wild beasts, but the names give no clue to their quiet behavior as they crawl the watery deeps. Presumably their markings have some resemblance to the markings of the animals they are named after.

Less ferocious beasts are represented by:
The Zebra Cowry, *Cypraea zebra* L., Florida-Caribbean;

The Giraffe Cowry, *Cypraea camelopardalis*
Perry, Red Sea;
The Rhinoceros Cowry, *Cypraea rhinoceros*
Souverbie, S. W. Pacific.
Close to this group, or with it, might be:
The Deer Cowry, *Cypraea cervus* L., West Atlantic;
The Little Deer Cowry, *Cypraea cervinetta* Keiner,
West Central America.

The Deer Cowry and Little Deer Cowry are both North American shells, the larger, perhaps, from off Campeche, East Mexico, and the smaller off Guaymas, West Mexico. The most beautiful and the largest Deer Cowry that I ever saw I secured in Campeche. I packed it in my soft pajamas, but later unpacked it in Cuernavaca, carelessly rolling the lovely Deer Cowry out on the tiled floor of my house, and cracked the shell all across the dorsum.

Among what might be called the small-animal group are:
The Cat Cowry, *Cypraea felina* Gmelin, Indo-
Pacific;
The Mouse Cowry, *Cypraea mus* L., North
Colombia to West Venezuela;
The Mole Cowry, *Cypraea talpa* L., Indo-Pacific;
The Tortoise Cowry, *Cypraea tetsudinaria* L., Indo-
Pacific;
The Calf Cowry, *Cypraea vitellus* L., Indo-Pacific.

Values of these cowries vary, but none of the Cowry Menagerie shells is rare or excessively expensive, except the Mouse Cowry, the habitat of which has not been too well known. The others are easily come by, and make a

pretty lot which I have not seen assembled by anyone.
Perhaps it is well to mention the birds also:

The Thrush Cowry, *Cypraea turdus* Lam., Indian
Ocean;

The Swallow Cowry, *Cypraea hirundo* Lam.,
Indo-Pacific.

Someday someone may collect the lot and set them up near the pictures of the animals for which they were named. If this ever happens I should like to see the unusual exhibit.

2O. WHAT IS A STROMBUS?

An unusual word is used as the name of a large group of shells which belong to the genus *Strombus*. In some of my earlier encounters with the problems of naming shells I searched back into the etymology of some shell names to see if I could trace through what had been in the thoughts of the persons who first gave names to shells and groups of shells. Very often the Latin will translate easily, and it becomes quite clear what the original namers of centuries ago had in mind. The word *astraea,* for instance, translates beautifully in the English word *star,* and it is quite clear at a glance that the species of this genus got the name because they look like stars. Similarly all shells of the genus *Conus* look like cones.

But the word *strombus* (pl. *strombidae*) is different. It is a hard-core word that dates back millenniums. Little light comes through as to what it orginally meant, or how it got going. It traces back to Latin, then to Greek, but it never seems to have had any meaning other than a name given to large shells. Perhaps it was used much like the word *conch* today, which is carelessly applied as a name for certain large shells.

My best guess is that the name is onomatopoeic, and that the sound of the word suggests something of the

20. Bull Conch (*Strombus taurus* Reeve).

robust nature of these shells. The *Strombidae* have certain general characteristics. Virtually all the shells of this genus are weighty for their size, and coarse rather than fine in their general texture and makeup. As an aid in identification it is worth remembering that all members of this genus have a thickened flaring lip, with a U-shaped notch, called the Stromboid Notch, in the lower part. This notch is used by the animal as a peephole.

The Fighting Conch, *Strombus pugilis* L., for instance, which is found in tropical waters of Southern Florida and the Caribbean, gets its name from its supposed quarrelsome propensities, although these fighting habits have been denied by recent observers. The *Strombidae* are noted for the antics of certain members of their species on the beach. There were reports from Florida, some years ago, that watchers, having disturbed several specimens of the huge and clumsy mollusk (called by the name of Queen Conch) on the beach at low tide, saw them flee in awkward leaps back toward the waterline. Most species of *Strombidae* live in shallow water from the tideline to a depth of about twenty feet. This would keep them within range of the food they prefer, for, in spite of their very active behavior, they are not carniverous, but live on plant material and detritus.

The foot of the animal is narrow and muscular, the operculum strong, sickle-like, and sharp. It serves not merely to protect against menacing crabs, but as a lever to help the creatures jump away to safety.

The weight of some of the shells of the *Strombus* family, such as the very popular Queen Conch, and the huge *Strombus galeatus* Swainson, of West Mexico, is so great that high postal costs make it impractical to mail specimens. This is one reason why collections of recent years often lack these shells.

Unlike other groups of shells, many of the *Strombidae* have been scientifically studied and reported on by top-ranking malacologists, among them Dr. R. Tucker Abbott, in Indo-Pacific Mollusca, a series published continuously by the Delaware Museum of Natural History. His monograph on Strombidae shows over fifty species on color plates, with supplementary insets in black and white. Among those shown are such collectors' favorites as *Strombus luhuanus* L., from the Indo-Pacific, with its reddish interior; *Strombus sinuatus* Humphrey, from Pacific seas, with its touches of purple; and the well-formed *Strombus granulatus* Swainson, which I often happen upon in little piles on the stands where shells are sold at Puerto Marques, near Acapulco.

Those collectors who strive for rarities will hope to obtain the exotic *Strombus taurus* Reeve, occasionally found in pairs by skin divers in the Marshall Islands.

21. PERIWINKLES

Although shell collectors value periwinkles as specimens, the human race in general regards them as comestibles. The ordinary East Coast Periwinkle, *Littorina littorea* L., rambles at less than a snail's pace about wharf pillars and coastal rocks. Like almost all Americans it is an immigrant. Abbott reports that it is not to be found among North American shell heaps or kitchen middens. It seems to have arrived from Europe, possibly on ships' bottoms, to Nova Scotia shores around the year 1800, about 100 years before I myself came on the scene to prey upon it. As a youngster I gathered them from the rocks, boiled them, removed the succulent morsels with a pin, and devoured them with relish.

Periwinkles have been a favorite food in Europe for a long time. They were sold in the streets of London as the roasted Pennywinkle. In the United States, overstocked as it is with easily obtained food, few people eat them. Actually they are a delicacy not to be overlooked or scorned. Current periodicals are continually prophesying impending world famine. Should this come about in the years ahead, we will look increasingly to the sea for food. Young people might do well to experiment in amateur sea farming.

21. Periwinkles (*Littorina littorea* L.).

The common periwinkle is about three quarters of an inch to an inch in size. It is brown to gray in color, and is circled with fine, irregularly spaced lines. It is excessively prolific. A century after its arrival on the American continent it had spread from Nova Scotia north to Labrador, and south to New Jersey, and had become the most plentiful univalve on our shores. Thus anyone near pure waters may gather a potful with ease.

M. S. Lovell, in his *The Edible Mollusca of Great Britain and Ireland, with Recipes for Cooking Them* (1854), gives the following piquant directions:

To Boil Periwinkles

It is only necessary to put them into a stew pan with as much water as will prevent the bottom from burning, as the liquid oozing from them will be sufficient for the purpose of stewing. When the shells open wide enough to extract the snail they will be adequately cooked. It should be noted that it is necessary to throw into the stew pan a handful or two of salt with the periwinkles, otherwise only part of the snail can be picked out.

Here is the recipe for Periwinkle Soup:

Take one and one half pints or a quart of periwinkles. Wash them well then boil them in a saucepan with a handful or two of salt to enable the snail to be picked out easily. Put a little dripping or butter into a saucepan with an onion or carrot with some chopped parsley and a spring of thyme, then fry until all is brown. Add a pint of water then as soon as it boils put in the periwinkles which have been picked from their shells. Add a little salt then let boil again for half an hour. It is simpler to boil them for five minutes or so. Eat them alone, or with buttered bread, perhaps with a cup of tea.

22. LOOKING FOR LAND SHELLS

Several years ago, when I was leaving for a trip to Mexico, Dr. Ruth Turner of the Museum of Comparative Zoology, in Cambridge, Massachusetts, suggested that I be on the lookout for land shells there. Land shells are a world in themselves, a world with which I was not too familiar. Nevertheless, my wife, Lorna, and I made quite a search from mountains to seashore. One of our first trips was into the hills outside Cuernavaca, at Loma de Atzingo, where a paved road up to a real estate development takes one up into cool pine forests. We sought diligently in the leafy undergrowth and under logs but our only reward was the sweet odor from the carpet of pine needles under our feet.

Our next search was at middle altitudes. A gardener told us that we might find some specimens in a spot he knew on the road to Cuautla, near the Canyon of the Wolves. So, on a Sunday morning, we drove ten miles east from Cuernavaca with the gardener and his son, who disappeared there into the wooded slopes. In an hour they returned, down-mouthed and empty-handed.

We made still another try, about the exotic plateaus at sea level near Acapulco. But still I found nothing. Acapulco and Cuernavaca are both based on hard rock.

22. Land Snails from Cuernavaca.

Hilly Acapulco rests, in its heat, on great masses of granite, whereas eternally cool Cuernavaca is on a slope of volcanic rock from such old volcanoes as Ajusco and Popocatepetl. These may not be good feeding grounds for land snails. They grow best where lime for their shells is easily available, and often in damp or wet places. In the end we were not entirely without success, however.

We were living in Cuernavaca in a delightful Spanish-type villa which we rent whenever our daughters are with us. It is perched at the very edge of a deep canyon cut perpendicularly down, with a stream of mountain water at a tremendous depth below. The gardener's children often played much nearer the edge of that deep cut than was safe, but their daring was not without purpose. One morning pretty Delfina arrived with a tin can of excellent live specimens of the robust snail in plate 22 (probably *Euglandina cumingii* Beck). They were not beauties, but they were large, about two inches along the shell. They proved so very active that we lost quite a few when they crept away in the night.

There are thousands of species of land shells. Locally they are just called snails. As they are native to most parts of the United States, they may be found there in any back yard or garden. In fact, they are found in virtually every country. The brighter-colored shells usually come from warm climates, as do the Cuban many-colored, orange-yellow and black-marked *Polymita picta* Born, once widely used in craft work but now, under Castro, politically scarce. Doubtless in time they will be back with us.

Some people might believe that the forms and colors of land shells make them more fascinating than seashells.

Species of beautiful form, and sometimes of striking color, are found scattered over all of the Philippine Islands, and in Fiji, New Guinea, and the South Seas generally. Famous collections are stored away and catalogued in the great museums of the world. But there are still species not known or studied.

It would be useful if those serving in the armed forces in tropical countries were to become interested in getting land shells from the native peoples, especially from the folk who come in from the country to the towns on market days.

Some years after our initial snail hunt in Cuernavaca, following a trip to the ancient ruins of Xochicalco, near Cuernavaca, I stopped by the side of the pavement near the circular lake, Lago de Rodeo, to enjoy the view. My friend Luis Herrera wandered off up the hill and in a short while returned with a handful of specimens of a small snail he had gathered from cactus plants. Later I took them to the Museum of Comparative Zoology at Harvard for identification. All they could tell me was that they belonged to a species of *Euglandina*. It seems that land shells may surprise us anywhere. A pupil of my wife, at the Vesper George School of Art in Boston, went diving in April, 1969, in a pond at Lakeview, near Boston, and brought her some specimens of the immigrant New England shell *Amphiperus malleatus* Reeve, well known in those parts for some years. It is said that this shell came from China, but it appears in Tetsuaki Kira's book on Japanese shells, so it may have come from Japan.

Another land shell, *Achatina fulica* Bowditch, the Giant

African Snail, has recently come into prominence in the eastern United States because, when uncontrolled, its vast depredations can make its presence a minor disaster. This snail is notable for its size, about that of a man's fist, and its appetite, since with its 80,000 sharp teeth it can consume a head of lettuce overnight. When introduced into a new location, free of its natural enemies, as it was in Miami, Florida and earlier on certain Pacific islands, the Giant African Snail multiplies so rapidly that a locality becomes alive with it.

It first arrived in the United States around 1947, on war equipment and cargoes after World War II, hidden in scrap, tires, pipes, and in the bodies of jeeps. It entered at San Pedro, and San Francisco, California. At Newark, New Jersey, forty live young snails were discovered and exterminated by being sprayed with steam, or by chemicals.

When the Giant African Snail arrived in Florida, several years ago, it had been traveling for a century and a half from its original home in the Island of Madagascar. It was brought in by a boy, as a present to his grandmother, after his visit to Hawaii. Laying about three hundred eggs at a time, it swarmed rapidly, and soon became a nuisance. A local official estimated that twenty thousand of the snails, with their colossal appetite for foliage, were to be found in one area only thirteen blocks square.

In its long pilgrimage, beginning in the early 1800's, it traveled first to mainland Africa, then to Mauritius. From there it was taken by conchologists first to India, later to Ceylon. It attacked rubber trees in Malaya, even sipping latex from tapping cups. In Ceylon it fed on tea plants. It was then deliberately distributed throughout Indonesia, to be crushed and used as a poultry food. When it reached Japan it was seized upon as a comestible and thus it reached Honolulu. In World War II the Japanese took it to supplement their rations on various Pacific islands, but when the war ended and American and allied troops took over, it was no longer eaten. It became so plentiful that these places were overrun. Jeeps skidded in the slime of crushed bodies.

In an attempt to control this pest of snails scientists studied it in Africa and found that there it was kept in control because it was eaten by humans, by civet cats, by land crabs, carabid beetles, and by another carnivorous snail called *goniaxis*. The *goniaxis* was then introduced into snail-infested Agiguan Island, in the Marianas, as a test. In four years the snails were conquered, their dead shells lying about in profusion, partly because they had eaten up all the available food supply. But scientists hesitated to introduce *goniaxis* into Hawaii lest it upset the balance of nature, so there the African Snail has been controlled by other means. It is proposed that in Miami it be kept in check by spreading a granular substance on the lawns. It has also been proposed that Americans eat it up, just as the Japanese did. Whether or not that will happen remains to be seen. Americans seem to lean too much toward steak and lobster.*

* A more complete account of the life and travels of the Giant African Snail, by Waldon R. Porterfield, may be found in the Milwaukee *Journal,* Oct. 10, 1969, p. 20. His account was the source of some of the facts reported above.

23. THAT EDIBLE LAND SNAIL

One of my wife's favorite dishes, when we were in Paris, was a plate of the snails known there as Escargots. Malacologically this snail turns up with the fancy name of *Helix pomatia* L. and it is something of a gourmet's treat in many parts of the world. Walter Freeman Webb, in his *Foreign Land Shells* (1948), tells us that this snail is common in Europe generally, where it is raised for the market and "fatted as we fat cattle." It is then exported frozen. One can get fried snails in New York hotels. I have also seen it on sale in cans, with shells included in separate packages, in fancy food stores in Boston and New York. It is not merely a modern comestible, having been prized as food for centuries well beyond the time for which we have written records. It has attracted more attention and has been more written about than other well-known shells.

Classical notations on *Helix pomatia* were written by E. M. da Costa, about 1776, and I quote his remarks from E. Donovan's *British Sea Shells* (1799):

> It is the largest species of land snail in England, and is found in hedges and woods. It closes its shell carefully against winter, with a white thick cover or

23. Edible Land Snails (*Helix pomatia* L.).

operculum, dull and like plaister, and in the closed state it remains until the beginning of April, or warm weather, at which time it loosens the border of the cover, and the animal creeps out of its shell for its necessary occasions. Dr. Lister informs us he kept one in his bosom about the beginning of March, when the animal, feeling the warmth, in a few hours disengaged its cover and crept out.

Da Costa continues his account with a description, taken from classical sources, of the Roman "stews," or snail farms, where snails were kept alive for table use.

The animal being large, fleshy, and not of an unpleasant taste, has been used for food in ancient times: it was a favorite dish with the Romans, who had their *cochlearia,* or snail stews, wherein they bred and fatted them. Pliny tells us, that the first inventor of this luxury was Fulvius Harpinus, a little before the civil wars between Caesar and Pompey. Varro has handed down to us a description of the stews, and the manner of making them: He says, open places were chose, surrounded by water, that the snails might not abandon them, and care was taken that the places were not much exposed to the sun, or to the dews. The artificial stews were generally made under rocks or eminences, whose bottoms were watered by lakes or rivers; and if a natural dew or moisture was not found, they formed an artificial one, by bringing a pipe to it bored full of holes, like a watering pot, by which the place was continually sprinkled or moistened. The snails required little attention or food, for as they crawled they found it on the floor or area, and on the walls or sides, if not hindered by the surrounding water. They were fed with bran and sodden lees of wines, or like substances, and a few laurel leaves were thrown on it.

Pliny tells us there were many sorts, as the whitish from Umbria, the large sort from Dalmatia, and the African, etc. This particular kind seems to be that he mentions. They propagate very much and their spawn is very minute.

Varro is scarcely to be credited, when he says, some would grow so large that their shells held ten quarts.

They were also fed or fattened in large pots or pans, stuck full of holes to let in the air, and lined with bran and sodden lees, or vegetables.

They are yet used for food in several parts of Europe, more especially during Lent, and are preserved in stews or *escargotoires,* now a large place boarded in, and the floor covered with herbs, wherein they nestle and feed.

In Italy, in many places, they are sold in the markets and are called *Bavoli, Martinacci,* and *Galinelle;* in many provinces of France, as Narbonne, Franche Comte, etc. and even in Paris. They boil them, says Lister, in river water, and seasoning them with salt, pepper, and oil, make a hearty repast.

This is not indigenous, or originally a native of these kingdoms, but a naturalized species, that has throve so well, as now to be found in great quantities. It was first imported to us from Italy about the middle of the last century, by a *scavoir vivre* or epicure, as an article of food.

Travelers of today might be interested in visiting local and foreign food markets to make a census of the modern snail population and investigate their sources both in the field and in whatever snail farms we may have with us at the present time. The industry of snail raising must flourish in some places, as the delicacy is still in favor.

24. THE CHITONS

Fascinating and astonishing are the ways of that small rock-climbing mollusk, the Chiton. Chitons compose one of the six definitely recognized biological classes of mollusks, the Amphineura, or Coat-of-Mail shells. It is not difficult to recognize a chiton shell, for, in spite of the large number of varieties, they are all similarly shaped—something like a narrowed turtle back.

R. Tucker Abbott reports that there are no more than three or four hundred species of chitons. They are found almost everywhere, for they are distributed from the icy northern seas to the warm shores of the tropics. About fifty kinds are found on the Atlantic coasts of the United States, while about a hundred live on the shores of its western coasts.

Most chitons are found on or under rocks, somewhere between tides. However, there are species that live in deep water. Some writers claim that these small creatures have something like a homing instinct, by means of which they always return from their short wanderings to the same depression or crevice in the rock.

Chitons are usually regarded as the most primitive or the simplest of mollusks, with only a vestige of brain, or no brain at all. The instinctive performance of very small

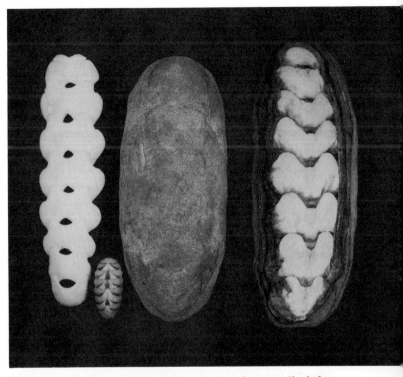

24. Chiton (*Amicula stelleri* Middendorf; without girdle [left];
with girdle, dorsal side [middle]; ventral side [right]; 1 1/3-
inch *Chiton lineata* shows relative size.

animals appears, at times, unexplainable, and so almost supernatural.

I recall one occasion when I removed several tiny leeches from a fresh water lake, put them on a nearby dusty road, and watched them turn with precision and inch their way, by some hidden inner drive, directly back toward the invisible lake shore. It is said that the instinct in some chitons goes so very deep that generations of a line going back into the distant past sought out and occupied the same rock crevices as their forebears, finding their own home spot through endless generations. This, however, I cannot vouch for by my own observation, nor am I quite sure how anyone else can.

The word *chiton* seems to be rather obscurely derived from the name of a Greek garment worn front and back over the shoulders. *Chiton* is roughly equivalent to the family name Amphineura, which means "having a sinew running around both sides." If this description is combined with the common name, Coat-of-Mail shells, we get a fairly good picture of a chiton shell.

It is an oval shell made up of eight movable parts or plates, the middle plates being squarish and the two end plates rounded off. Circling these is a tough, leathery band, called the girdle, which holds the plates together, and acts as a contractile muscle. All this equipment protects the soft animal on the inside of the domed oval, enables it to cling like a suction cup to a rocky surface, and to curl up into a ball when touched, or in danger.

Chitons make an admirable collection. There are quite a few of them, and they vary in size, color, and design. Some of them, like the two in plate 24, present an attractive appearance. The small one, *Tonicella lineata* Wood, is cream colored, and beautifully patterned with reddish lines. It is found from Japan to the Aleutian Islands, and south to San Diego. The three larger shells shown in plate 24 are all the same shell, the Giant Pacific Chiton, *Amicula stelleri* Middendorff. It is found from Japan to California and is probably the largest of the chitons, normally six to twelve inches long—a very striking shell.

Plate 24 also shows the oval back of this chiton (center). Next to it (right) is the bottom side of the same shell, showing how its skeleton is held together by the muscular girdle. On the other side of it is the removed skeleton. The plates are fastened together, after curing, by an adhesive, without which they would fall apart. Josiah Keep, in his out-of-print 1888 classic, *West Coast Shells,* (referring to the plates) says that these single valves are found much more often than the complete animal and from their peculiar shape are called butterfly shells.

Collectors looking for chitons will find them on and under rocks in tidal areas. They cling hard to surfaces and must be pried away, when they may immediately curl up, to the collectors' confusion. Dr. I. Mc. T. Cowan tells us, in the January, 1964 issue of *Pacific Northwest Shell News,* what to do about this, and how best to preserve any color. He suggests preparing the specimens without any chemical or heat treatment. Specimens may be fastened to wooden sticks, and allowed to die in unaerated fresh water. The cleaned specimen may next be bound flat on a stick, dried out, and buffed with mineral oil, then added, as one more fine specimen, to one's collection.

25. THE COWRIES

So fascinating are the cowries that some enthusiasts keep drawers full of the beautiful and variable Tiger Cowry, *Cypraea tigris* L. This shell is probably the most populous of the larger cowries and so is easy to come by. Many people, perhaps most people, own at least one in their lifetime and sooner or later, it is said, one may be found as a bit of debris or decoration in almost every house in the land.

The Tiger Cowry is plump and opulent, and the colors so intriguing that collectors often place specimens of this shell in groups of contrasting colors, some almost brown, others almost white, and some with a line of red or a splotch of blue. A color photograph of such a group is becoming almost fashionable. Of all the families of shells, undoubtedly the cowries hold sway as prime favorites. They are hoarded by some like jewels.

But the Tiger Cowry is merely the seed of a collection that may grow and grow. Among the first sought after by enthusiasts are some of the larger cowries. One of the most liked is the Eyed Cowry, *Cypraea argus* L., named after Argus, the son of Zeus, who had many eyes, some of which were always awake. The circle "eyes" spotted on the light brown cylindrical shell make an unpredictable

25. Cowries. ROW I, FROM LEFT: Map Cowry (*Cypraea mappa* L.); Ivory Cowry (*C. eburnea* Barnes); Chinese Cowry (*C. chinensis* Gmelin). ROW 2: Lamarck's Cowry (*Cypraea lamarcki* Gray); Reeve's Cowry (*C. reevei* Sowerby); Chestnut Cowry (*C. spadicea* Swainson). ROW 3: Boivini's Cowry (*Cypraea boivinii* Kiener); Jester Cowry (*C. scurra*); Beautiful Cowry (*C. pulchra*).

pattern. Equally coveted is the Map Cowry, *Cypraea mappa* L., with its pattern of lines, among them its dorsal line resembling, to some, a map, but to me seeming more like a plant stem with its branching leaves. The Tortoise Shell Cowry, *Cypraea testudinaria* L., appears like the back of a cylindrical tortoise. Dark brown with its markings, it is sprinkled with white dots as if it were powdered.

Next in choice might be the spectacular Mourning Cowry, *Cypraea mauritiana* L. Colored over the back in lovely shades of brown, it is banded around the base with its mourning black. Oddly, its Latin name, given it by Linnaeus in the days when localities were but sketchily known, refers to the Island of Mauritius. Who knows but that it owes this name to a misplaced label? Somewhat scarcer ones are Friend's Cowry, *Cypraea friendi* Gray, from West Australia, with its color patterns often patched with blue, and the Australian *Cypraea hesitata* Iredale. These, and all other cowries, are shiny and appear as if brightly polished or lacquered. Doubtless this adds to their charm in the eyes of those who seek them.

After the sizable cowries come a raft of little fellows, some plentiful, many scarce. First among these is the fabulous Money Cowry, *Cypraea moneta* L. In terms of its performance as a shell, not as a comestible, this is the most remarkable of them all. Coin of the realm, money, cash, whatever you like to call it, this shell has been a medium of exchange among Indo-Pacific peoples, from the distant past even, perhaps, until today. Strings of them, piles of them, buckets of them have been used to buy and sell.

The picture in our minds of black men, brown men, white men, yellow men bargaining and bartering in the pale or golden Money Cowry throughout the ages makes us wonder how a tiny shell can possibly become money. Here we become abstruse. To be money, the thing so used must appeal to humans, must be available but scarce in quantity and, most important of all, must be accepted by the people concerned as a medium of exchange. We men of today put our trust in paper printed and issued at the whim of our rulers. We may well ask how often modern peoples have been left with useless paper money. The German mark of an earlier day? The Chinese yuan? If inflation ultimately sweeps our own modern paper currencies into the garbage can, the humble Money Cowry will still be worth some monetary equivalent.

How can I name here the hundreds of small cowries which lure and delight the lover of shells? To mention just a few, there are the jewel-like Onyx Cowry, *Cypraea onyx* L.; the slightly larger Chestnut Cowry, *Cypraea spadicea* Swainson; the Calf Cowry, *Cypraea vitellus* L.; Cox's Cowry, *Cypraea coxeni* Cox; the Swallow Cowry, *Cypraea hirundo* Sowerby, its synonym being *Cypraea ursellus* Gmelin; the omnipresent Serpent Head, *Cypraea caputserpentis* L.; the tiny Chick Pea Cowry, *Cypraea cicercula* L.; the unique Dawn Cowry, *Cypraea diluculum* Reeve; the white-banded Foal of an Ass Cowry, *Cypraea asellus* L., used for the eyes of old-style idols before we turned our worship toward the more ephemeral flicker and flash of today.

26. MORE ABOUT COWRIES

As the cabinets and plastic drawers of the avid cowry collector begin to fill up, and not too many new species become available, he may turn his attention to special races or strains, each with its own particular name. Aided by those malacologists called "splitters" by some,* we may trace down sub-species or races of the same cowry, specimens found in seas far apart and so appearing in slightly different patterns. Walker's Cowry provides a convenient example. From the Indo-Pacific comes *Cypraea walkeri surabajensis* Schilder, from one part of Australia comes *Cypraea walkeri continens* Iredale, and from another part of Australia comes *Cypraea walkeri comptoni* Gray. These strains differ but slightly from one another in markings, but these small differences appeal to some, for reasons too complex or too obscure for easy explanation.

Certainly a subject for unending conversation is that group of elusive shells known as the rare cowries. Top

*Those scientists who are humorously called "splitters" prefer to divide shells into many groups, giving a different name to each. Others, called "lumpers," like to group many shells together under one name. Would it be correct to call the Schilders (F. A. Schilder and M. Schilder) splitters and R. Tucker Abbott a lumper? Here is a subject for conversation.

26. Some favorite cowries. ROW I, FROM LEFT: Little Beauty
Cowry (*Cypraea pulcella* Swain.); Ivory Cowry (*C. eburnea*
Barnes); Groove-toothed Cowry (*C. sulcidentata* Gray);
Verco's Cowry (*C. verconis* Cotton & Godfrey). ROW 2:
Daybreak Cowry (*Cypraea ziczac diluculum* Reeve); Tesselated
Cowry (*C. tesselata* Swain.); Sieve Cowry (*C. cribraria* L.).
ROW 3: Blunt Cowry (*Cypraea stolida* L.); Mouse Cowry (*C.
mus* L.); Cox's Cowry (*C. coxeni* Cox).

conversation piece is the so-called Golden Cowry, *Cypraea aurantium* Gmelin, which, though attractive, is far from golden in appearance even if golden in price. I have nothing to add to what is written elsewhere in this book about that will-o'-the-wisp. (See pp. 78–81.) I have seen poor ones, dull and pale with age, but few good ones, fresh, unblemished, and unfaded in color. Look critically at your specimen, if you ever get one, or preferably before you get one.

Several other cowries are much rarer, though less touted, than the Golden Cowry. You may peek at a color illustration of some of them on the cover of the second edition of Van Nostrand's *Standard Catalog of Shells* (1967). Or you may see some of them listed as rare in S. Peter Dance's book, *Rare Shells* (1969), where he offers the history of fifty specific specimens of choice rarities. One species, long lost, recently came to light when a scientist in Arabia discovered the locale of *Cypraea teuleri* Cazanavette at Museera Island, about a hundred miles from Muscat. In March, 1969, he sent out a fisherman who returned with a small harvest. He then got in touch with a few reliable shell dealers in the United States and netted some cash to help put his children through college. The shells found were quickly sold to eager buyers in Mexico, Italy, Belgium, Australia, and the United States for about two hundred dollars each. Some of the specimens are pale and lightly marked, others have dark dorsal patches like the one shown in plate 26, photographed by my wife. Many more have been found since, so specimens are no longer rare.

Just now a friend of mine has been offered the Great

Spotted Cowry, *Cypraea guttata* Gmelin, for $1,000. At the same time another friend is being offered one for $2,000. Up to now neither of the victims has succumbed, but the first one is weakening and I am sure he will have his specimen before this goes to print.

I might mention as very rare Fulton's Cowry, *Cypraea fultoni* Sowerby; the Brindled Cowry, *Cypraea valentia* Perry; and *Cypraea langfordi* Kuroda. In matters of price for such shells, if ethics are involved, they are involved but vaguely. The collector's motivational drive and the amount of his cash reserve are intermingled in determining what he is willing to pay. A price is what a thing is worth to you.

The lore of the Cowry is vast. Cowries have been used for many and various purposes, almost more than we know about. They have been used for personal ornamentation, as when a lace of white shells has been strung across the dark forehead of a woman; for decoration, as in India, making a frontal piece on the head of an elephant. Women today still use cowries in brooches and rings. The Usambra tribe of East Africa used them as a charm against evil. They were sacred to the Omaha Indians, who placed one in a shrine. They have been used in death rituals, and certain tribes stuffed them in the mouths of the dead. Most of all, cowries have been used, as in the Pacific Islands, for food. These various uses have been written about in more detail in my book *Gems of World Oceans* (1964), so I do not feel justified in repeating what was written there.

Some happy authors, writing in such works as the *Encyclopedia Britannica,* like to dwell on the fact that certain cowries resemble the female genitalia. They go on from there to tell how primitive people have draped themselves with belts and amulets made from cowries in the hope of stimulating whatever gods there be of human fertility. Such reports may be true but, as I view the large and often pitiful families of the world's poor people, I wonder if such charms are really needed.

27. WEST COAST ROCK SHELLS

Some years ago shells from the West Coast of Africa were almost unobtainable. At that time I had long been trying to get the elusive West African Horned Murex, *Murex cornutus* Lam., to match one in my wife's collection. Imagine my surprise when I learned, from one morning's mail, that a friend in Oregon had just received only one from Angola, and that it had already been mailed to me.

Surprise and anticipation are part of the excitement of being a collector of shells belonging to any of the large groups like the rock shells, or *Murex* shells (pl. *Muricidae*), of which there are hundreds of species in temperate or warm seas in a belt around the world. A number of attractive shells in this genus are found on the East Coast of the United States from Florida to the West Indies. Some of these are the Lace Murex, *Murex florifer* Reeve, and the rare Beau's Murex, *Murex beaui* Fischer and Bernardi.

Over a dozen species are found off the American West Coast; of these, four favorites are shown in plate 27. These are all somewhat colorful and spectacular shells from the warm waters of Mexico's West Coast, that land of fabulous ocean playgrounds. They are the Root Murex, *Murex radix* Gmelin; the Cabbage Murex, *Murex brassica* Lam.; the Pink-Mouthed Murex, *Murex erythrostoma*

27. West Mexico Rock Shells. ROW 1, FROM LEFT: Root Murex (*Murex radix* Gmelin); Cabbage Murex (*M. brassica* Lam.). ROW 2: Pink-mouthed Murex (*Murex erythrostoma* Swainson); Black Murex (*M. nigritus* Philippi).

Swainson; and the Black Murex, *Murex nigritus* Philippi.

Rock shells are all more or less rough and spiny, with raised ribs or varices, and so are in marked contrast to the cowries, which are all smooth, round, and glistening. Whether they were originally called rock shells because some of them look like a rock, or because some are found among rocks, would be hard to tell, although I incline to the latter view. For the most part they have a rough, globe-shaped body-whorl, a low spire, and a definitely observable canal at the end opposite the spire.

In many attractive species this canal is much longer than the global body of the shell, as in the Snipe Bill, *Murex haustellum* L., the Venus Comb, *Murex pecten* Lightfoot, and the Giant Venus Comb, *Murex troscheli* Lischke. These, and a number of others, are ornamented with long, sharp spines, which may shoot out erect, like thorns, all over the shell.

Virtually all *Muricidae* are decorated with scales, spines, sharp points, horns, or spikes. It is, perhaps, this processing in great variety that makes them fascinating. Just why are they so curiously formed? Presumably there is an element of self-protection in this aggressive growth-behavior, since enemies might find the spines somewhat fearsome, scarcely an inviting morsel for a fish to swallow. Accidentally, in the Chicago Public Library, I once ran across a small book by Johannes Kepler, in which the great 16th-century scientist concerned himself with the matter of form in nature. Kepler came to the conclusion that natural forms are not always purposeful, or directed toward a practical end, but are also directed toward ornamentation. Perhaps creative imagination in nature expresses not merely the urge to survive, but also a striving to beautify or entertain. That is my personal belief.

In terms of survival, it has been noted that the more lacy and spiny shells live among coral or in relatively protected places. The big, boulder-like species are found on rocks or in deep water, where their greater smoothness protects them from the beating of the waves or the pressure of heavy currents.

The four shells shown in plate 27 are all of this latter type, found in the rough coasts or deep waters off West Mexico. These four shells are among the all-time favorites of collectors. Each has a considerable size, so that it can be easily handled and well displayed as a single ornament or in a collection. Each makes a fine showpiece because it features a color pattern that can hardly fail to impress.

No shell of any size that I am familiar with shows anything like the sharpness of color contrast in black and white that makes two of these shells so striking in appearance. The Black Murex, *Murex nigritus,* lives a bit north and seems to be confined to what the Mexicans call the Sea of Cortes. (This appears on English-language maps as the Gulf of California.) The younger specimens of these shells are almost white, but they add black as they grow larger, reaching about six inches. This shell is often confused with the similar Root Murex, *Murex radix,* which grows farther south to Ecuador. It is a rounder, solider shell, with overlapping spines, and it looks like a knobby root. Both of these black-and-white shells live on reefs, feeding mainly on clams. They force open the two valves of the clam and suck out the nourishing juices.

Brassica means "cabbage," and the *Murex brassica*

might be regarded as resembling that vegetable because of the lacy, leaflike processes on the body-whorl. But the shell is far more beautiful than a cabbage. Cream-colored and chunky, it is banded with brown, and in fine specimens, especially younger ones, the tips of the lacy decoration of the shell are touched with pink. Large shells, with rich pink about the opening, may grow to eight inches, but such specimens are scarce.

A great favorite of collectors is the Pink-Mouthed Murex, *Murex erythrostoma*. It has a bright pink enamel facing around the aperture and shows pink inside the whole, giving the appearance of an opening rose. Smaller specimens with poor color are plentiful. But the shell grows to about five inches, and fine, rosy-enameled specimens of good color may come from deep water, and so be relatively scarce.

After all my references to the rock shells, it may be surprising to find out that *Murex* really means "a marine animal from which purple dye is extracted." Perhaps this is because the famed purple used to dye the robes of kings who anciently wore the royal purple came from the glands of a rock shell whose Latin name is *Murex brandaris* L., a little shell that looks like a small *Murex cornutus*.

28. DYE FROM SHELLS

Anyone willing to take a little trouble can color a piece of cloth with dye extracted from a shell which he may be able to pick from the rocks on the nearest shore. Children used to do such things in school, and when life returns once again to the elementary school doubtless they will do so again. The common Dog Whelk, *Thais lapillus* L., and several related shells generally called Purples (or *Purpura* shells) have a gland which secretes a liquid from which dye can be made. Some *Muricidae,* among them the famous dye shells of the Mediterranean and certain *Purpura* shells found on American coasts, have also been a source of dyes in the days before other dyes became more practical.

A thousand years before Christ the cities of Tyre and Sidon, situated in what is now Lebanon, throve on an industry which gathered shells, crushed them, and from the fleshy parts extracted Tyrian Purple, prestige color of the ancients. A. Hyatt Verrill, in his *Shell Collector's Handbook* (1950), reports that a pound of such bright-colored wool was worth over two hundred dollars. Because this coloring was so highly valued, purple became the royal color and it remains so, symbolically, in the robes of princes and prelates today.

28. Classical dye shells. FROM LEFT: *Murex brandaris* L.; *Murex trunculus* L.

Two common Mediterranean shells, *Murex brandaris* Lam. and *Murex trunculus* L., were used to fabricate this dye. Piles of the old discarded shells, comparable to the American Indians' kitchen middens, are still to be found in Italy. The process of dye extraction was as follows.

When the flesh was removed from the broken *Murex* shells the remains were soaked in salt water. This extract was boiled in a lead kettle and strained, leaving a clear, pale green liquid. Wool soaked in this and dried in the sun turned a dull purple. After washing in a weak lye solution or in soap and water, however, it was transformed into a lovely, permanent carmine or magenta, not exactly what we call purple today.

In a similar way a purple dye may be extracted from certain intertidal shells variously called *Buccinum, Thais,* or *Purpura* Shells. Commonly called Dog Whelks or Purples, their distribution is so wide that they may be found on the coasts of England and on the east and west coasts of the United States. I have often gathered *Thais lapillus* at low tide at various places on Cape Ann in Massachusetts. On the West Coast may be found the common whelk, *Thais emarginata* Deshayes.

In his classic 1799 work, *British Sea Shells,* E. Donovan wrote as follows about the extraction of dye from a shell he called *Buccinum lapillus,* the "Massy Purple Whelke."

> These shells are found in great abundance near low-water mark, on many of the shores of Great Britain. It is one of the species that yields the purple dye analogous to the purpura of the ancients; and though the value of its dye has longe been superseded

by the cochineal insect, the shells that produced it are objects of curiosity. The Tyrian purple was the most admired, and is known to have been extracted from a species of the Murex; but other purples of inferior lustre are also mentioned by the ancients. Da Costa imagines that the liquor of this Whelke, *Buccinum lapillus,* was a valuable purple to the ancient English, and quotes the authority of Bede, who lived about the seventh century, for his opinion. "There are," says Bede, "snails in very great abundance, from which a scarlet crimson dye is made, whose elegant redness never fades, either in the heat of the sun, or the injuries of the rain, but the older it is, the more elegant."

One other source of purple is a shell called *Purpura patula pansa* Gould. Mexicans on the Gulf of Tehuantepec dipped threads of cotton textile in the milky excretion. Skirts made of this dyed cotton were costly and had their own special name, *decarocollio.*

29. THE CAPE COD SCALLOPS

Cape Cod is the center of a scallop industry which nets New England in the vicinity of ten million dollars a year. The famous shellfish involved are the Deep Sea Scallop and the Bay Scallop. These two edible bivalves provide the population of the United States with one of its favorite delicacies. The whole soft part of the scallop is edible, but the only part customarily marketed and eaten is the white circle of pure muscle. This, since it is attached to the inner side of both halves of the shell, serves the creature to open and close its valves, and so to dart about in jet fashion in the water in remarkably nimble movements.

A fleet of ships is kept busy seeking out the shells, cutting out the muscles, and preparing for market the colossal yearly crop. The ships are equipped with dredges composed of a network of steel rings of a size which drops smaller shells and picks up those of the right size. The nets scrape the sea-bottom of St. George's Bank, off Massachusetts, for the large Deep Sea Scallop, *Pecten magellanicus* Gmelin. These scallops are opened at sea and the shells thrown overboard.

Other boats work the Cape Cod coasts for their catch of the smaller Bay Scallop, *Pecten irradians* Lam. According to law these must be brought ashore whole, and are

29. Center: Deep-Sea Scallop (*Pecten magellanicus* Gmelin);
four corners: Bay Scallops (*Pecten irradians* Lam.).

opened in fishing huts near the water's edge by amazingly skillful and rapid workers. The shucked shells and unusable inner parts of the mollusk are dumped in hillocks as refuse. The parts thus thrown away are many times the volume and weight of the white, succulent morsels sold as scallops.

Scallop shells, of which there are many world varieties, are of considerable interest to shell collectors, some of whom specialize in scallop collections. From the collector's point of view, the two main species of New England scallops, especially those chosen shells which are of unusual marking or color, are attractive and desirable as specimens.

Why is it, then, that these beautiful shells are not plentiful and visible in every collection? Simply because a scallop shell consists, not of a single valve or plate, but of a matched pair, fitted together tightly and exactly at the edges. Because of the customs of the shellfish industry, such matched pairs are scarce.

Although thousands of the scallops are caught each year, matched pairs of shells are exceedingly hard to come by because the two valves are separated at sea, and thrown overboard separately. After the steel dredge drops its big catch on the deck, the crew members open the scallops one by one, remove one valve, and throw it overboard immediately. They then cut out the muscle from the other valve and discard this second valve, probably into a pile of them on deck.

Interfering with this habitual routine would, naturally, be irksome. Thus it is that only by special arrangement is it ever possible to get any of these beautiful shells. If you are ever fortunate enough to obtain a pair it is worth displaying against a background of white absorbent cotton so that the pink globe of the shell may be seen to advantage.

The fishermen bring their catches of the smaller Bay Scallop ashore in canvas sacks. They fill a huge basket with the separated shells, after opening them, and dump the whole in an ever-growing heap. A collector's one hope of getting good matched pairs, even if he is right there on Cape Cod, is to benefit by the good will of one of the fishermen and ask to search through the contents of a basket of discards.

Shells of the Bay Scallop, although graceful in form, are usually drab in color, especially when covered with the slime of the mollusk and the grime of the sea. The trick is to seek for the needle in the haystack, the other valve! An hour or two more, working with a chlorine bleach, acid, and vaseline, and you will have a set. A good collection of Bay Scallop shells may range through all-white, yellow, orange, and spectacularly marked black-and-white specimens. It is something to be proud of, for it makes a most attractive display.

30. SHIPWORMS

There is a mollusk so small and obscure that most people who have been very close to it have never seen it. Yet its impact on the human race has run into billions of dollars. It is known as the Shipworm, or *Teredo* (pl. *Teredines*).

Shipworms, which are not worms, have from time immemorial caused incalculable damage to sailing vessels and the wharves where they dock. Their ravages continue, for they are all-time trouble makers for men of the sea. In 1964, the replica of the ship *Bounty* built for the film *Mutiny on the Bounty* was sailed from its West Coast berth to be moored as a show-vessel at the New York World's Fair. In the course of its long journey through tropical seas it fell afoul of shipworms and was so badly damaged by them as to be in danger of complete ruin.

When the seriousness of the situation was realized a desperate call came in to Dr. Ruth Turner, famous Malacologist of the Museum of Comparative Zoology in Cambridge, Massachusetts, a leading authority on shipworms. Dr. Turner was able to explain the problem and advise methods for its solution, including the use of certain modern chemicals. As a result, the *Bounty* was saved, and safely docked in its basin at Flushing Meadows.

Plate 30 shows a small piece of wood picked up on the Cape Cod beach, riddled by *Teredines*. The small holes

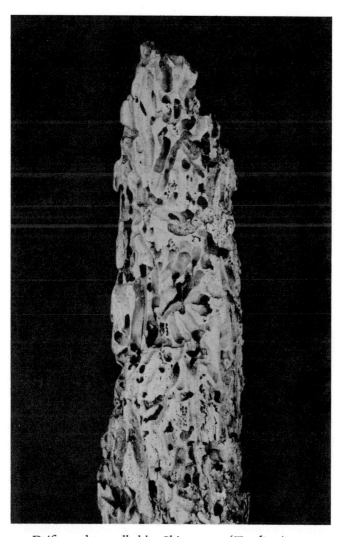

30. Driftwood tunnelled by Shipworms *(Teredines)*.

over and through it are not so innocent as they appear. To look at them one would hardly believe that the whole interior of the wood is honeycombed with long channels lined with a shelly substance, homes for the long, worm-like mollusks which had bored into the wood.

That these invaders were mollusks was long unknown. They were unrecognized as anything but worms. Their life was a mystery. Not until 1733 did Godfrey Sellius study the situation and announce that the so-called ship-worm was actually a bivalve mollusk. Later study has revealed its peculiar life history.

Teredines, or shipworms, all begin their lives when set free from their parent into the ocean currents. The larvae settle on whatever wood they find, creep about by means of a tongue-shaped foot, and begin their work.

The tiny bivalve shell is small in relation to the size of the long, wormlike process it develops. The animal possesses two sets of what are revealed under the microscope as fine, filelike teeth. The foot adheres to the wood, the body begins a rocking movement, and the rasps saw away at the wood, reducing it to fine dust, and opening up a channel for the mollusk to live in. The wood dust is cleared away by being swept into the mouth and from there passes into the stomach. There, presumably, it is acted upon by digestive ferments and, along with various microorganisms, seems to serve as food.

As the channel lengthens, the "worm" enters the wood. It scrapes out a burrow long enough for its growing body, which ends in plates of shell material forming the two valves. The burrows may grow to an amazing length, as much as twelve inches, in temperate seas. In tropical waters they may reach the enormous length of six feet.

As it enters the wood, the long body trails behind it. Two siphons extend to the outside surface of the wood, making possible the entrance of the respiratory current of water. At the outer end of the long body is a pair of paddle-shaped plates, "pallets." These can block the opening and shut off the interior creature, closing its door.

There are several species of shipworms which are named *Teredines,* the best known being *Teredo navalis* L., found on the coasts of the United States, Europe, and Africa. The *Teredo* known as *Bankia gouldi* Bartsch is found on both the east and west coasts of America.

On the West Coast the destruction caused by an outbreak of *Teredo* infestation in San Francisco Bay injured jetties and wharves to the tune of $25 million in one four-year period (1917–1921). This unusual plague was caused by the fact that these shipworms thrive in water of a certain limited salinity. Heavy rains had reduced the amount of salt in the Bay, allowing the shipworms to live closer to the shore than before. On another occasion the wood dikes of Holland were riddled, and they began to crack up; the country was almost inundated.

Teredines still pose a problem. Some attempt is made to control them with creosote, with which wharf pillars are soaked or painted. Other chemicals recently developed are found to be partially effective. The Greeks and Romans used metal shields on the hulls of their ships. Copper sheathing was used in the 18th century, and metal sheathing and concrete protection are still used today in an attempt to conquer what will probably always be a problem for shipowners.

31. SCHISTOSOMIASIS

Freshwater snails are said to be responsible for infecting 200 million people a year with schistosomiasis, a serious sickness. The parasites which cause the illness penetrate the skin of children and adults, usually while they are wading or bathing. The names and distribution of the snail-borne organism are given in *Merck's Manual of* [Medical] *Diagnosis and Therapy* (Merck & Co.: Rahway, N.J., 1966) as *S. haemotobim* in Africa, the Middle East, Spain, and Cyprus; *S. mansoni* in Egypt, the East and West Indies, and the northern two-thirds of South America; *S. japonicum* in Japan, Central China, the Philippines, and Celebes. The *Manual* adds that *S. mansoni* is often found in Puerto Ricans living in the United States. Infection is also possible outside these areas. It has been claimed that one might be affected by eating watercress sandwiches in England.

Symptoms and development of the disease are something like this. If a person swims in polluted waters and is infected, he may at first suffer from a skin irritation at the spot where the parasite entered. The infecting organism may then pass into the liver, bladder, intestinal wall, or other tissues, breeding there and so causing various discomforts and serious disturbances. Medical treatment is complex and tedious.

31. Schistosomiasis-carrying mollusk species: *Oncomelanis mesophora* Robson (smaller specimens); *Phyopsis africanum* Krauss.

The significance of schistosomiasis is no mere individual matter, however. It has tremendous social and economic importance. Many overseas industrial and military operations are disturbed by a group incidence of the disease. Millions of lost man-hours affect the work forces.

The social and financial losses which ensue have been of concern to the World Health Organization. Large sums of money are being contributed and spent to support the study of this and other mollusk-borne diseases, their prevention and control. Such studies have led to the development of a special branch of science called medical malacology. This has its own specialists in a few universities, and is taught as a definite area of study.

Some of what is written here reached me through a lecture given by Dr. Edward Michaelson to the Boston Malacological Club. Dr. Michaelson is a member of the staff of the Harvard Medical School. After skillfully outlining the problem of illnesses caused by mollusks he reported what is being done to solve that problem.

Dr. Michaelson described the way in which schistosomiasis is transmitted to man as follows. Certain species of snails are infected by the parasites, and their eggs are excreted into freshwater streams, where they hatch out. The living organisms enter the skin of humans, and are passed by waste to others, sometimes affecting whole groups.

Fantastic and somewhat garbled stories are told of the disastrous ravages of schistosomiasis. One account in a newspaper claims that a third World War was narrowly averted when a huge Chinese army, readied to attack Formosa and assembled in the Yangtze River Delta, became incapacitated by this sickness. A whole work-force was laid low in an asbestos mine in Tasmania. A television documentary once reported that a British regiment in Nigeria was debilitated by infection from snails.

Huge amounts of money continue to be spent on intensive research, partly motivated by startling prospects. Aswan Dam in Egypt, for instance, may become a mixed blessing because of these snails. While the resulting irrigation can redeem much arable land, produce vast new crops, and so increase the food supply and save many lives, even more lives may be disturbed by schistosomiasis carried by snails infesting the new waterways.

It proved difficult for me to obtain specimens of infective snails to photograph. The specimens shown in plate 31 were kindly provided for me by Dr. William Clench of the Harvard Museum of Comparative Zoology. Of the schistosomiasis-carrying snails shown, the small specimens are *Oncomelanis mesophora* Robson, type locality Katayama, Japan. The larger snails are *Phyopsis africanum* Krauss, collected by A. Loverage in the Greek River, Uganda, in 1933.

32. BIG AND SMALL

To a man as big as a mountain an elephant would be tiny. Man is the point of reference in the universe and many things are arranged just to suit our size. An orange fits the hand; an egg or two, our appetite for breakfast. We judge the size of all things by reference to ourselves, as if we considered ourselves central to the universe. Size affects us in curious ways, so that few of us who would kill an ant would shoot an elephant. Is it important to kill a horse and nothing to boil out a periwinkle?

Size being relative to our own size, we have large shells and small shells to collect and display. Usually people are first attracted to large shells, since they have greater visibility. A controversy still rages as to whether or not the East Coast Gulf of Mexico Horse Conch, *Fasciolaria gigantea* Kiener, which can reach a length of two feet, is the world's largest univalve. Its rival is the Australian *Syrinx aruanus* L., once called by the delightful name of *Megalotractus proboscidifera* Lam. This shell also grows to two feet, and at this size is so heavy it is seldom seen in the United States. I have heard rumors that this Australian shell holds the edge for size, but I await exact statistics before awarding the pennant.

Among other shells of generous size are two from the

32. Giant univalves. *Pleuroploca gigantea* L. (left); *Syrinx aruanus* Kiener (right); 1 1/4-inch Onyx Cowry (center) shows relative size.

East Coast of the United States, the big Queen Helmet, *Cassis madagascarensis* Lam., and the Great Conch or Pink Roller, *Strombus gigas* L. These are mentioned elsewhere in this book (see p. 299), but here it suffices to say that these may well be the big boys of the collection, centerpieces to stand out and hit the eye. The Giant Clam is so immense we seldom see large pairs, since their very weight makes shipment difficult. Occasionally a single valve is made into a birdbath, or is used as a baptismal font. I know one kitten that curls up snugly in a favorite half.

As to small or tiny shells—these exist in myriads. Whole groups of smallish shells must be neglected in this book because of the tedium involved in trying to list or identify them. Mere mention can be made here of whole families and groups of shells on which some worker could concentrate all his efforts. The Olive Shells, sleek and shiny, will keep anyone busy for a long time, as will the Star Shells, which include the spectacular *Guildfordia yoca* Jousseaume, and the yellow-and-blue-touched Star of Stars, *Astraea stellare* Gmelin. What can we say of the limpets, suction cups of the rocks, except that they are plentiful at the shore; or of such tiny beauties as the purple *Janthina janthina,* the pagoda-like *Columbarium pagoda,* the sculptured *Drupa* shells, the little *Natica, Nassarius,* and *Nerita* shells, the bright-colored Strawberry Shell, *Clanculus puniceus* Philippi? These are for collectors who have special affection for small shells. Tiny shells are not difficult to acquire, but they are hard to identify, and will give a long lesson in patience to anyone who cares to learn from them.

There are some few who collect the tiniest shells, some almost like powder, which they keep in phials and look at with a magnifying glass. Such sands of the sea are too minuscule for presentation here. Here, however, is a project for anyone who will embrace it. In their book *The Shell* (1963) Hugh and Marguerite Stix magnified some medium-sized shells into giants by enlargement, revealing hidden beauty in them. So the tiniest shells, enlarged by photography, can still reveal a world as yet unseen.

33. LONG AND THIN

I do not like to write an uninteresting paragraph if it is possible to avoid doing so. I must confess, however, that as I approach the subject of those thin, pointed shells, the Miter Shells, the Augurs or Screw Shells, and the Spindle Shells, I am confronted with a wall of the banal and the commonplace. The miters provide a modicum of interest, since the imaginative Linnaeus, who named some of them long ago, thought that in their spires he saw a resemblance to the tall headdresses of Churchmen. So we may start at the top of the hierarchy with the Pope's Miter, *Mitra papalis* L. from the Indo-Pacific. It has a well-delineated crown and is, appropriately, splotched with red. It is a beautiful shell and its original name remains in usage. Not so, however, with the similar but smoother Episcopal Miter, once called *Mitra episcopalis* L. The favored name today is *Mitra mitra* L. The Pontifical Miter, *Mitra pontificalis* Lam., was so called for about a century until someone checked it through in malacological records and discovered that it had been earlier named by the English conchologist H. F. Link, who called it *Mitra stictica*. Imagination still had play here, as the shell was presumably named after Sticte, one of the hounds belonging to the mythological hunter Actaeon. (Actaeon, who had

33. Long, thin shells. FROM LEFT: *Turritella terebra* L.; *Terebra triseriata* Gray; *Mitra taeniata* Lam.; *Terebra maculata* Lam.; *Fusus irregularis* Grabau.

incurred the wrath of the gods, was changed into a stag and torn to pieces by his own hounds.)

There is a general rule that a name which has held for a hundred years need not be changed, even though the shell involved had been named by an earlier writer, but it does not seem to apply here, and it seems that collectors can choose for themselves among the various scientific names. Personally, I prefer the more colorful ones. Looking up the exact history of a name is for a professional who is bound to scientific accuracy.

At this point I digress from the main subject, long thin shells, to discuss the general matter of naming. I feel very strongly in the matter of personal freedom in labeling one's own shells with any proper scientific name preferred by the owner. In the articles written by aspiring amateurs, who seek, as we all do, to buttress their egos, do I detect a certain pride in an attempt to use the most recent or fashionable name? Is it common sense to be thus too punctilious? Any name, once given and correctly published, with a sound description, should serve as a good label, or as a name used in a published book or article, especially if a recent name change has caused confusion. The reason for this is that all scientific names are on record somewhere in malacological literature. If one has any one good name for a shell, all its names can be traced in malacological records by anyone who has the time and training, and who has access to a museum library.

I still get shells from Tanzania labeled *Pterocera aurantia,* a name attached to the picture of this shell in one of Webb's books. I may leave it as it is, or I may change it to *Lambis crocata* Link, a more favored name. In any case it is definitely the same shell, and we collect shells, not names.

To resume the main theme—there are many miter shells, and as a group they are popular. Among the most liked are two from West Mexico, the Peace Miter, *Mitra zaca* Broderip, and Belcher's Miter (named after Captain Belcher of the *Sulphur*), *Mitra belcheri* Hinds, both sizable. Then there is the lovely, rare bright-orange-banded *Mitra taeniata* Lam. from Australia, and the Queen Miter, *Mitra regina* Sowerby, from East Africa, with banding of red, orange, and yellow. Among the less attractive miter shells there are so many species that you can collect a drawerfull, and find them difficult to name unless they come to you correctly labeled. Photographs of a goodly number of them appear in Walter O. Cernchorsky's *Marine Shells of the Pacific* (1967).

The Augurs, or Screw Shells, are also in some variety. Called by the generic names of *Terebra* and *Turritella*, they are thin, sleek, pointed, and fanciful. Many of them are from Indo-Pacific waters. Most popular of the *Terebridae* is the Marlin Spike, *Terebra maculata* L., so called because very large specimens look like marlin spikes and are heavy enough to brain a man.

Two of the well-known augur shells are difficult to distinguish from one another without a careful look. *Terebra subulata* L. has two bars of squarish dark dots; *Terebra muscaria* Lam. has three rows of square, brown spots on each whorl. A secondary ring distinguishes it from *Terebra subulata*. Unique is the three-terraced *Terebra triseriata* Gray, thin and needle-like, and the Crenulated Augur, *Terebra crenulata* L., ringed by brown dots and white knobs. A *Turritella* is like a *Terebra* in shape, but has a different aperture. *Turritella terebra*, from the Philippines, is a much-liked species, and *Turritella goniostoma* Valenciennes is a large representative from West Mexico.

Somewhat different are the Spindle Shells, long, but swollen at the aperture, tapered crown above and longish tail or canal below. Generally they resemble *Fusinus couei* Petit, from East Mexico, and *Fusinus dupetit-thouarsi* Kiener, from West Mexico. They all tend to be whitish or grayish, and of a dull finish.

The shells referred to in this section are too much admired to be entirely left out of a book like this. Such a grouping is in no sense scientific, in fact it is malacologically absurd. But I suspect that few malacologists will read this book, for this is a popular treatment written for a wider audience. I am content, therefore, to let its unorthodoxy remain a secret shared with any of my readers who have found my words interesting enough to carry them to this point.

III

CURIOUS AND
INTERESTING

34. EXPENSIVE RARE SHELLS

Rare shells present something of a puzzle. In the first place, it is difficult to obtain a rare shell, and hard to find a person who has discovered one and is willing to part with it. Such shells usually come from relatively inaccessible waters. If no one seeks them, they will not be found.

General events affect the supply of rare shells. For example, until recently Japanese pearl divers and others visiting the warm waters off northern Australia sometimes found rare shells in the course of their work and brought them in for sale. Then these divers left to work in other fishing grounds, so that the unusual *Volutidae* they had been bringing in almost disappeared from the market for a time.

Another matter that affects rarity is that some mollusks seem to exist in relatively small numbers, as if they were a dying race. This might be so of the shell shown in plate 34, *Cymatium ranzanii* Bianconi, over $6\frac{1}{2}$ inches long, which came from waters off East Africa. Collected off the northern end of Cabeceira Peninsula, in 6 meters of water, it was discovered in a narrow channel in a seaweed area which was strewn with coral boulders. In the same habitat were seen *Lambis truncata, Harpa major,* and *Conus bandanus.* The waters teemed with fish—parrot fish, sturgeon, and barracuda.

34. *Cymatium ranzanii* Bianconi.

When this *Cymatium ranzanii* arrived it was the first and only one I had seen. It was said to be the twelfth known specimen. The eleventh, over eight inches long, was reported to have been sold for $800. Since that time I have seen only one other live-caught specimen, and the shell remains rare.

Cymatiums are not as much coveted as some other species. Had it been a cowry or a volute shell, equally rare, it would have commanded a higher price. The shell shown in this chapter, acquired by a distinguished Florida collector, won recognition in an annual exhibition as the Shell of the Show.

With its particularized locality data, this shell is just as rare as ever. Nevertheless, some months later, several of this species appeared on the market from another locality, and at a lower price. It seems that some diver had discovered, in a habitat not known before, a small "nest" of these shells. Temporarily there was a price drop. But since the diver who discovered the new habitat may have cleaned out all the specimens clustered there, they will not breed, and might become even scarcer than ever. Who knows?

It should be obvious that nothing in the appearance of this shell would indicate that it is very rare. It looks much like several other Cymatiums, and quite like *Cymatium tigrinis* Broderip, a scarce shell from western Central America. Only a sophisticated collector would recognize *ranzanii* as a rare shell. Its value does not come from its appearance but from its unavailability.

It is reported that the price of diamonds is regulated by a central commercial control, which helps to keep the market relatively stable. No such control exists for rare shells, although they are much rarer than diamonds. Diamonds are in steady supply, but there is no steady supply of rare shells. They are not available on demand from the sea. In fact purchasing them is something of a gamble. It is unlikely, however, that any of the really rare shells will ever become commonplace, or available in quantity like the Tiger Cowry or the Money Cowry. On the other hand, there is some likelihood that certain rare shells will become scarcer and so rarer than ever, because they cease being found. Just which shells will become rarer, and when, will only become known as time marches on.

35. SPIRALS

The way in which shells grow in spiral forms is remarkable. Many of us collectors have wondered about this, and so have myriads of people before us. To some extent it is a mystery. But an understanding of the mathematical and natural forms of the spiral as they occur throughout all nature does somewhat clarify the matter.

The figure in plate 35 shows what is called the logarithmic spiral. A fuller discussion of this is in my book *The New Culture* (Reynal and Hitchcock: New York, N.Y., 1937). The spiral begins at a point and increases outward with mathematical regularity. A glance at the diagram will immediately remind one of the spiral form shown in the interior of a split Nautilus, one which has been sawed apart to show the interior chambers.

These spirals are not exactly the same, however. For it seems safe to say that the spirals found in the tendrils of a sweet-pea, in the form in which the seeds appear in the head of a sunflower, and in thousands of seashells, are never simple mathematical spirals. They are subtle modifications which make each natural thing unique.

Each spiral in nature is specific to the plant or shell concerned. It is reproduced in generation after generation in exact, distinctive form by forces which are little under-

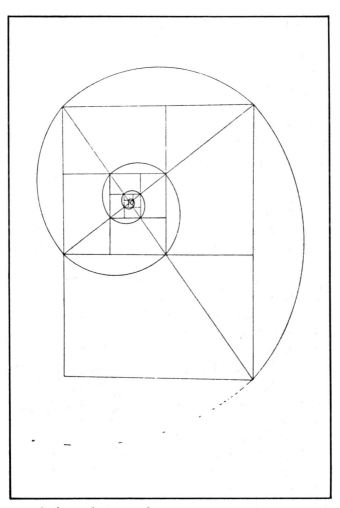

35. The logarithmic spiral.

stood, and little investigated by scientists. There is a science of form, morphology, but it is little pursued in recent years.

My own interest dates back many years to a summer in London. My wife and I had reading cards in the British Museum so while she examined the original of the Lindisfarne Manuscript I looked for unusual books. At that time we were both interested in the spiral forms appearing in such masterpieces as Botticelli's *Birth of Venus,* in which Venus is shown born from a seashell, and in natural forms of plants and shells.

It was a real discovery for me to find two books, now long out of print, by T. A. Cook, *Curves of Life* (Constable and Co.: London, 1914) and *Spirals in Nature* (John Murray: London, 1903). Anyone really interested in spirals as they appear in art and nature, and especially in seashells, would enjoy these unusual books. From a study of them it could hardly fail to become clear that there is a spiral-forming force operating to move the living being through time and space. As the seashell grows, it has a force of life behind it, projecting it into growth and maintaining it in time from its beginning until it reaches normal size. Since this process continues from birth to death, the creature moves through both time and space.

A flat spiral (shown on p. 169) does not fully indicate such growth, and it is better symbolized by a spiral in three dimensions like a watchspring pulled out from one point to a wider circumference. The beginning point of the spiral stands for the life force. The movement through space symbolizes growth. And the enlarged spiral shows that life goes on in a fourth dimension of time.

Seashells go through some such process of growth. Beginning with a point of life, say the egg, as in the Channeled Whelk, they continually deposit lime into a shell moving in complex spirals as the shell grows slowly, larger and larger. The interior of a shell, sawed apart, will often show the central pillar around an imaginary axial line, and reveal to the imagination the way the shell has grown.

Slowly and deftly it continues on its own pre-designed form of growth, taking on its own peculiar inherited pattern, increasing in size day by day and season by season. It adds its lime particles, deposited from the fleshy parts, as if the granules of lime were strung out like beads on the invisible trellis of a field of magnetic force. In such a way all shells are formed in spirals, moving through time and space, their solidified forms appearing as the deposits of lime make each individual shell.

36. PATTERNS

The way in which shells develop, or are put together by nature through growth, is a continuing mystery. Although many collectors have reflected on it, and a few have studied it, at best all we have are fleeting glimpses of the truth.

Perhaps the simplest way to think of things or atoms being put together is to recall the method used by a child, with single building blocks, to make a house; or, similarly, to think of a number of uniform red bricks that are added regularly to one another until they become a wall. In architecture this is called the modular method. In it each building block or brick is a unit.

C. H. Waddington states this same thing, in serious and perhaps more difficult form. He says the idea of the module covers two related notions. The first is that of using some standard unit of length or volume as the basis for the whole design. The second is the adoption throughout the design of a single set of proportional relations. (See Gyorgy Kepes, *Module, Proportion, Symmetry, Rhythm* [George Braziller, Inc.; New York, N.Y., 1966], p. 20.)

It is obvious that shells are not grown, or put together, by any such simple method as that of sticking marbles or pellets of dough to one another to form a three-dimen-

36. Rhythmic patterns on Bednall's Volute (*Voluta bednalli* Brazier).

sional pattern. Anyone who likes to do so may try this himself and see if he can get anything that looks like a shell.

There are, nevertheless, definite forms and also surface patterns, growing as the shells grow in some complex way dictated by the genes. Shells express symmetry but are sometimes bisymmetrical. They also express rhythm and subtlety of pattern.

To follow out these thoughts easily just look at the photograph showing the rare *Voluta bednalli* Brazier, one of the loveliest of shells. It sometimes comes from the vicinity of Thursday Island, north of Australia, and generally is priced in the vicinity of $150. The shell shown at the upper right of plate 36 appears in another book written by me. I had very much wanted to include this shell in the book but had been unable to secure one. It came in at last, so late that the photograph had to be pasted on the plate just before the book went to press.

Some years ago I met with a group of thoughtful friends led by the late superb poet, Anna Hempstead Branch, in her Poets' Guild Room at Christodora House, in New York's downtown East Side. Wondering whether any observable principle runs through all the creative activity of art and nature, we concluded that this common element was rhythm. Rhythm may be thought of as movement forward in pulses of alternating long and short, like that of a wave. It seems that all shells exhibit this characteristic of rhythm, which appears beautifully, as if etched, on the surface of Bednall's Volute.

This effect of rhythmic growth seems to be there in all shells. The rhythm or beat is never simple. The Nautilus

Shell and most bivalves are bisymmetrical if cut by a single plane. But shells like the Lambis or the Spider Shell are not. In any case, the growth movement, impelled forward by the little-understood forces of life, produces complex forms and patterns passing themselves on from generation to generation.

In shells like the Eyed Cowry, *Cypraea argus* L., this surface design is composed of many circles and dots in a pattern always recognizable, but never exactly the same. It gives the effect of random balance. Such patterns are never simple regular repetition, like the designs on wallpaper.

Perhaps such meditations, even if they do not help us to understand fully the process of shell formation and decoration, nevertheless give us some basis on which to appreciate more fully the beauties of form and pattern so lavishly displayed in shells. To a large extent these beauties seem to be the basis of their charm.

37. SILVER SHELL

The simulated shell shown in plate 37 came from China. It is a very unusual object, unusual because of what it is, how it came into my possession, and what it seems to mean. Its exact purpose, or how it can possibly have come into being, is a mystery. It is made of silver, chased and partly overlaid with a spiral in yellow and blue enamel, and is fashioned as a pendant locket topped off by an eyelet, or loop, so that it can be suspended by a chain. In all probability it is an original, the only one of its kind, made by a silversmith on special order from an individualistic Chinese scholar. I came by it as follows.

It was my good fortune, toward the end of the first quarter of this century, when China was still open but little known to Western travelers, to live there for two years. It was like a dream to be there, yet it is more of a dream as I look back upon it now. It is hard to realize that I was ever there, but this is proved by my possession of the shell locket I bought in Peking.

One day, as I was wandering outside the Chien Men, a gate between the two walled squares of Peking, I found my way into what was then (and perhaps still is) called Flower Street. On this narrow alley, flanked by the fretted wood fronts of Chinese shops, was a famous

37. Silver shell from Peking.

jewelry store which I had visited once before. To step into that shop was to enter a world of amazement and delight. The show space was merely two small, plain rooms, but the side walls, the shelves, and the cases set about the rooms were filled with a thousand objects of silver and gold, of rose quartz, lapis lazuli, and white-and-green jade.

Had I known then what I know now, instead of spending the few dollars I could spare, I should have pawned some of my possessions from the West, and bought what took my fancy. I did not find out for years that the stock of such curio shops was largely made up of loot from the imperial palaces, stolen in the riots and upsets which took place in Peking early in this century.

In those days the Peking shops were full of fabulous works of art which could be bought for a song. Only when I returned ten years later to Peking did I find them gone from the shelves, never to be replaced. But, although I was both ignorant and poor, the moment I saw the silver seashell I knew I must have it for my own.

At that time I spoke a little Chinese, which I have since almost forgotten. Without showing any anxiety, I priced the shell, along with some other pieces. I no longer remember the cost, but it was very small. Soon I left with my shell, along with a cut-silver shield with a pink coral frog at center, and a few rings of marvelous design. The other trinkets have long since been given away as presents. But the shell I have kept because it is so very full of meaning.

Looking at this silver locket, you will see that it is shaped like a clam shell—not any actual clam shell, but a generalized one as seen by an artist. Inscribed on the colored enamel outside each valve is a clear and definite spiral. To the artist and philosopher this is always a creative symbol of generation. The two valves of the shell open on a hinge and, as it is activated by the opening of the shell, there swings into place the figure of a man, hanging free-moving in the form of a cross, supported by the hands.

Obviously this bit of shell jewelry is a symbol. A symbol is something designed to speak without words. But to be understood it must be read by each person for himself as he sees it. To me it seems that this small shell is saying that all living things are impelled through life, through time and space, by the force of creation, which by orderly processes develops into its highest form, man. But whatever philosophy is read into it, or out of it, the shell leaves us to explain, as best we know how, the origin of life.

The silver shell points up a question posed on every side by every form of natural life. In the end, however, we ourselves must answer the question, each man as he has been taught, and as he sees for himself.

38. FRILLS AND FURBELOWS

Even after some years of familiarity with seashells you do not cease to wonder about their shapes and forms, which account, among other things, for their never-ending appeal.

The cowries, for example, are extremely smooth, rounded and shiny, sleek and handsome. Why? At the other extreme are the rock shells, or *Muricidae,* with their remarkable, proliferating processes, or projections, each form characterizing a distinctive species. Here again, much as we may wonder at the forms taken by these shells, no clear answer comes to mind.

The shell in plate 38, the Branching Rock Shell, *Murex ramosus* Lam. from Pacific seas, is an excellent example of frilly processing. It is a very popular shell, wanted for most collections because of its vigorous appearance, and for its often pure-white color, with pink staining on some of the branches of the most attractive specimens. It has an abundance of half-spinelike, half-leaflike curling processes which are characteristic of many of the *Murex* shells.

Some of the most startling examples of this processing are to be found in several much-admired species. One of these is the prized three-to-four-inch Rosy Murex,

38. Branched Murex (*Murex ramosus* Lam).

Murex palma-rosea Lam., from the Indo-Pacific. This shell has its own unique shape, and is noted for the faint rose color on some of its rather profuse frilling. The rose color, however, is not an identifying mark because many fine specimens are without it.

The Deer Horn Murex, *Murex cornucervi* Bolten, with an alternative name of *Murex monodon* Sowerby, from northwestern Australia, is usually dark brown, though sometimes paler, with darker, often almost black, rather lavish processes. It has a unique black curl proceeding from the "tail." This tends to curl back over the body-whorl, and actually does so in the more fanciful specimens. I know of no other shell which has this interesting phenomenon. In the best specimens this curl is well developed, making the shell something of an oddity. Both the Rosy Murex and the Deer Horn Murex are on the scarce side.

Frills and furbelows are by no means limited to the *Murex* shell family. The frilling of the Furbelow Clam, *Tridacna squamosa* Lam., plentiful in Pacific seas, is notable. When it first arrives uncleaned it looks a bit rugged. But a few hours' cleaning and filing may reveal lovely lemon or orange coloring, and the remarkable hooding and ribbing which give the shell its common name.

An unusual little bivalve, which our family calls the Pastry Shell, is the Venus Clam, *Callanaitis disjecta* Perry, also called *Venus lamellata* Lam, from southeast Australia. The frills on this bivalve move in two directions and converge in a way hard to describe. A shell from New Zealand which resembles it is the Venus *Bassina yatei* Gray, the two making an interesting pair.

Again we keep asking: Why do shells have these spines, curls, branches, and furbelows? The first answer that comes to mind is that the device of spines and processes is protective. Such shells might appear to a hungry fish very hard to swallow. But when we think of the smoothness of the cowries, which gives them no spiny protections, and when we realize that many rough shells are found in the stomachs of fish, this answer—that spines and processes are protective—seems little more than a poor speculation.

Nature does not always seem purposeful. On the contrary, it seems endlessly playful. It produces forms in crystals, plants, and animals so varied, and often so lovely, it is hard not to believe that they are the products of a creative imagination which expresses itself in a universe intended to intrigue and delight human beings down through endless millenniums.

39. A CONE SHELL SAYS "HI!"

There are few shell collectors who do not have a special corner for what might be called curious shells. Collectors are always on the lookout for such shells, which add considerably to the interest of their acquisitions. Fortunately, nature does not machine-process her gifts, so all natural things appear in intriguing variety. Seashells are no exception. A collector can never order an exact size, shape, or pattern for a shell. Many collectors do, however, ask for a shell "just like the picture."

Each of the five cones in plate 39 is strictly one of a kind. Before reading the following lines you may prefer to scrutinize each shell in the photograph to see if you can discover its peculiarity of marking. The shell which is clearly marked with the salutation "*Hi*," the stocky, rather heavy cone to the left, is a *Conus augur* Hwass, from Zanzibar. Its cream-colored background is always banded by a series of indiscriminate, dark markings which may resemble a script of some sort and so justify its name as the Augury Cone. This Cone seems to augur good fortune by proclaiming the cheerful greeting "Hi!"

If "Hi" is appropriately followed by an exclamation mark, this is to be found on the cone to the right. It is a specimen of the Japanese *Conus sieboldi* Reeve, a fair-

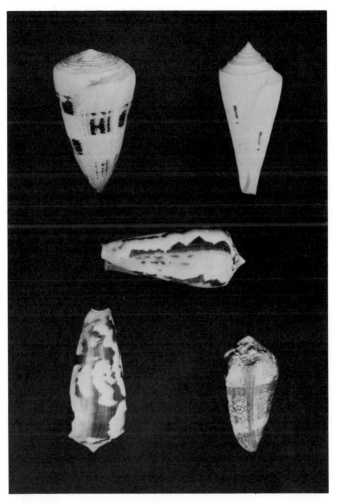

39. Oddly marked Cone Shells. ROW 1, FROM LEFT: *Conus augur* Hwass; *Conus sieboldi* Reeve. ROW 2: *Conus gubernator* Brug. ROW 3: *Conus gubernator* Brug.; *Conus praelatus* Brug.

sized white cone usually lightly sprinkled with a few faint, miscellaneous markings. The exclamation point on this one is emphatic.

In the center, below the *Conus augur* Hwass and the *Conus Sieboldi* Reeve, and also below to the left, are some very interesting specimens of the glamorous *Conus gubernator* Brug., the Governor Cone, from Mozambique. A good *Conus gubernator* is a thing of beauty. The patterns vary in the most attractive fashion and a number of specimens of this shell, seen together, are quite fascinating to look at and compare. Against the whitish background appear flecks, and figures as well as assorted fantastic markings covering the whole body-whorl of the shell.

The color of the markings on *Conus gubernator* varies from light coffee-brown to almost black. On some of the cones a lavender painting or tinting looks as if it were washed in about the dark patterns. The seascape on the one in the center forms an attractive vista. The figure on the other specimen (below left) may seem to resemble a seahorse.

The remaining shell is a specimen of the Prelate Cone, *Conus praelatus* Brug., also from Mozambique in East Africa. It seems to be something of a coincidence that the Prelate Cone should be the one on which a cross can be clearly seen. *Conus praelatus* is in some ways one of the most attractive, certainly one of the most unusual, of the cones. It is one of the group called tented cones because the markings look like a series of tents of different heights lined up in rows. Its unusual appearance is due to the fact that, although some specimens are brownish, it is usually suffused with a wash of blue against black, the tented markings, looking very smart indeed, well warranting the name Prelate Cone.

The markings on all these cones are varied and beautiful. The one shown in the photograph, however, is the only cone shell I have ever seen that bears its own Sign of the Cross.

40. COLOR IN SEASHELLS

It is natural to like seashells with lots of color. Yet gay color is not really an outstanding characteristic of most seashells. Except for the whites, grays, and browns, colors are found in relatively few species.

Some people take a fancy to certain shells because of their color, and most collectors want a number of brightly colored shells to pick up the general appearance of their shell displays. Among the favorites are shells which feature some particular coloration on one part. Some of these are listed below:

Selected specimens of the Pink Murex, *Murex bicolor* Valenciennes, from West Mexico, if they are taken from deep water, have a shiny pink frill about the opening which makes them resemble roses.

The Cameo Shell or Bull Mouth, *Cassis rufa* L., which comes from East Africa, has a deep stain, almost blood-red, about the opening. Red is found also in the little Strawberry Shell, *Clanculus punicea* Philippi, and in a very different shade in the Harp Cardium, *Cardium lyratum* Sowerby, from Pacific seas.

Indeed a number of cardiums combine attractive shape and color, as does the large, five-inch yellow *Cardium elatum* Sowerby, from West Mexico.

40. Bright orange Noble Scallop (*Pecten nobilis* Reeve).

Orange-red markings occur on some of the miter shells, *Mitra papalis, episcopalis,* and *pontificalis.*

A lavish peach-color brightens the lips and wide aperture of some of the Melon Shells, like *Melo indica* Gmelin, and *Melo amphora* Solander.

The huge Pink Roller or Queen Conch, *Strombus gigas* L., has always been a much-wanted shell. Brought ashore in Florida, the West Indies, and East Mexico, it has been, for many years, a notable ornament in American homes, flaunting its wide pink opening in many places as a decorative piece, a hanging flowerpot, or even in a row of border pieces along paths or garden beds.

Probably the prize shell for color, the very brightest of all, and among the few that even approximate the overall color of garden flowers, is the Noble Scallop, *Pecten nobilis* Reeve, from Japan. Even in its common colors, from deep reddish to red brown, it is a lovely shell. But the scarce bright-orange specimens are probably the most bright colored of all seashells. The rarer, rich clear purple specimens are beautiful shells, especially when shown side by side with the orange ones.

Not too much is known as to the causes or processes by which a shell paints itself with color, or what makes rich color, and what tends to dull or pale. Generally speaking, it is thought that shells in cool northern or southern waters, and from deep waters, tend to be rough and pale. Shells in warm tropical waters, and those in shallower water where light may reach them from the sun, seem to have the most color.

The food consumed by shells (that is, its abundance and its nature) is believed to affect color. But basically color is a matter of biochemistry which scientists are beginning to study more fully. The methods by which mollusks extract color to lay in their shells, and just why some members of a species are one color, while others are another (as different as purple and orange) remain entirely a mystery. On the other hand, although we have black cats, white cats, and tiger cats, we do not bother to wonder about that. We just accept it.

There is considerable scientific knowledge of the way in which color is fed into the shell by its soft, fleshy inhabitant. More technical accounts may be found in scientific works on shells. Generally speaking, it is enough to say here that glands in the fleshy part of the shells are specialized to lay in color.

The same specialization in patching and banding found in the shell is also found in the fleshy part of the animal which deposits the lime of the shell form. The color is laid into the lime when the creature deposits the solid particles in the marvelous process of shell formation.

The science of malacology is continually advancing and, as biochemical studies are carried on by a new generation of marine biologists, we shall look for more information on the fascinating matter of color in shells.

41. SEASHELL RAINBOW

When I was young one of my few good teachers taught me a mnemonic for the spectrum, using the initials of the sentence; "Run, you great big Irish villain." This helped to spell out red, yellow, green, blue, indigo, and violet. As to intermediary colors, orange color, which appears in some shells, falls somewhere between red and yellow and is seen in certain special strains of *Turbo petholatus* L. from the Philippines. Pink or rose color is seen in the bivalve *Tellina perieri* Bertin, from Japan.

Following through the spectrum in shells, each color might be represented by the following:

BRIGHT RED, a bit on the purple side, is found in a bivalve, *Cardium lyratum* Sowerby, often from the Sulu Sea, in the Philippines. Dark red appears in the much-admired Strawberry Shell, *Clanculus punicea,* which comes from Mozambique, East Africa, and looks like a small strawberry.

YELLOW coloring, in a great swollen bivalve, is found in the lovely five- to six-inch *Cardium elatum* Sowerby, from western Mexico. Lemon yellow, probably the purest bright yellow in shells, is seen in the rare, high-priced special specimens of the Noble Scallop, *Pecten*

41. Well-knobbed Lion's Paw (*Pecten nodosus* L.).

nobilis Reeve, also notable for bright orange and purple specimens. It comes from Japan. Yellow also appears in the rare color-form of the nodulous Lion's Paw, *Pecten nodosus* L., from Florida. Such shells used to come in from sponge divers in Tarpon Springs, Florida, but they are getting scarcer and scarcer.

GREEN is a scarce color. The only bright green shell I that know is the Emerald Snail, *Papuina pulcherrima* Rensch, found only on Manus, one of the Admiralty Islands. Seashell collectors often make an exception of this one and add it to their collection as a color accent. It is one of the few shells that are as brightly colored as the feathers of a macaw.

BLUE to INDIGO are unusual colors in shells, but are seen in the abundant Common Mussel, *Mytilis edulis* L., found all along the northeast coast of America. Vast beds of mussels were, until recently, found even along the shores of downtown Boston, although the last time I looked for them there they had been scooped away as some obscure result of the press of human crowds. Generally speaking, when people advance, seashells retreat, and no wonder.

When I was a child we climbed out on huge rocks at Prince's Lodge on Bedford Basin, Nova Scotia, where my father had a summer home, a place where the water was clear and unpolluted. We waded in and freed the huge mussels from their hairy byssus and used them for food, watching for an extra bonus of lovely pearls, sometimes found in the soft, fleshy mantle. I have seen sailors from French warships gathering these mussels off Halifax to use in a luxury meal on ship. A more aristocratic shell, in some specimens touched with blue, is the Prelate Cone, *Conus praelatus* Brug., from East Africa, a tented cone shell of more than usual beauty.

BRIGHT PURPLE is found in the small snail-shaped *Janthina janthina* L., pelagic in the warm seas of the world, and sometimes found off Florida. It floats on the surface by means of a raft of bubbles. Commonly called the Violet Snail, it brings us to the end of the rainbow.

42. SHELLS FOR
WINDOWPANES

Some shells seem to surround themselves with special interest because, in one way or another, they have appealed to the human imagination, or have become associated with human living. Two such shells within the same genus, and so related, are the Saddle Shell and the Windowpane Shell.

They have become much tangled up in their Latin names through the years, but both of them are usually called by the generic name of *Placuna,* which means "a plaque." They are both flat, platelike bivalves, although the mature Saddle Shell is a bit wavy in shape. Both are plentiful in seas extending from the Philippines to Australia.

The Saddle Shell looks like a saddle. In some books it is called *Placuna sella* Gmel., an appropriate name since the word *sella* means "saddle." These bivalves, which are a bit clumsy to handle, live buried in the mud. They are large, sometimes reaching eight to ten inches across, and half an inch thick, the two flaky valves fitting tight, like those of an oyster or a scallop.

Young saddle shells are flat, smoky pearl inside, and semi-transparent. Since, in early life, they are much like windowpane shells, they are similarly used. But as they

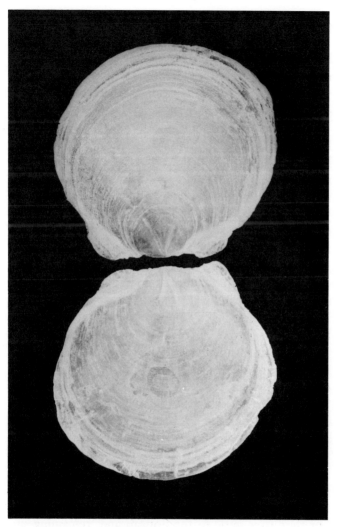

42. Windowpane Shell (*Placuna placenta* L.).

grow larger they take on their typical, odd saddle-shape.

Some scientific authorities do not favor the name *sella,* but use the name *ephippium* Retzius. This name does not mean "a saddle" but "a saddle-cloth," or caparison. One will have to put two labels on this shell to secure both scientific approval and picturesque accuracy!

The Windowpane Shell, a common species in the Indo-Pacific, has been, and still is, widely fished in the Philippine Islands. Its name, *Placuna placenta* L., does not mean windowpane, but comes from the flat shape of the shell. It is the largest of its genus, and is said to be the thinnest of bivalves in relation to its size. Because it is so very flat it has been named *placenta,* which comes from the Greek for a flat cake, or other flat object. (The word *placenta* is familiar in English, since it is used to refer to the flat vascular mass attached by the umbilical cord to supply nourishment to the human fetus.)

Because the shells are unusually flat, and also translucent, they have been widely used as windowpanes. These mollusks usually live close to shore, and thrive mostly on muddy or sandy bottoms in salt-water bays, or estuaries where there is some inflow of fresh water. They live on microscopic marine organisms, such as diatoms. The mollusk inside the shell breathes and eats by raising its right valve partly above its left valve, allowing the entrance of currents.

The sexes are separate, both sperm and eggs being cast into the water, where fertilization takes place. At first the tiny young float about freely in the oceanic currents, but they later settle to the bottom and, remaining unattached, lie in the mud on the sea floor. They do not burrow but use their muscular feet to keep mud from entering the gills. Large crops of the shells lie in beds on tidal flats.

Windowpane shells are so prolific that they soon replace themselves with a fresh colony if the beds are depleted temporarily by poor living conditions. Some windowpane shells are found dead in deeper water, but large quantities can be collected live by simply wading in at low tide, locating specimens with fingers or toes, and pulling them out.

The dull, micalike valves are whitish outside, silvery purple within. Because of their transparency and delicate pearly luster, these shells are much in demand for making craft objects such as lamps. Attractive hanging mobiles are sometimes made from them. For hundreds of years the shells were used by Chinese and Filipinos for windows. Before World War II shell windowpanes were to be seen in some of the churches of Manila.

Before World War II there was also a large industry in these shells. It was controlled by Chinese who had arrangements with local fishermen to deliver the cleaned crop to them for sale and distribution. Later, it is said, better conditions were given to the workers by Americans who took over and directed the trade.

Several million windowpane shells were used annually in house construction and shellcraft and to some extent are still so used. Some of the more peculiar uses have presumably disappeared, since seed pearls, found clustered in the shells, were once ground and used both as medicines and for face powder.

43. SHELL MONEY

Seashells, cut up and strung together in cords, served as money to build up the capital used by a Mr. Prince to start a real bank in the state of Maine. Shell money, often called wampum, had been used for thousands of years by the American Indians before the arrival of white men. When the Europeans came, they adopted shell money from practical necessity in order to deal with the Indians.

It became the standard currency for the colonists. At first they obtained all their money by trading with the Indians for wampum. The colonists standardized the value of this money at four shillings, or about one dollar, for a length or fathom of the blue or purple wampum. This money was made from the Quahog Clam, *Venus mercenaria* L., shown in plate 43, and eaten in New England as the Cherrystone Clam.

Seeing an opportunity to make money, Thomas Prince, an early governor of Massachusetts, took things into his own hands. At that time Maine belonged to Massachusetts, and Prince secured sole rights to the manufacture of shell money in Maine. This he was permitted to do without any backing for the money in gold or other types of security.

A machine had been invented to cut and grind wam-

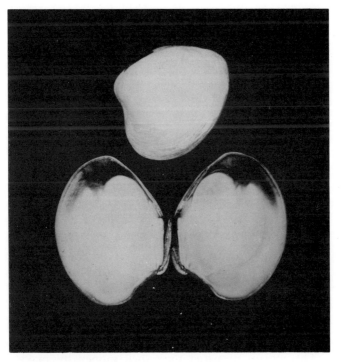

43. The Quahog Clam (*Venus mercenaria* L.).

pum. All that was necessary was to secure a stock of shells from coastal parts, hire cheap labor, and turn out the money in quantity. Mr. Prince then dreamed of using this money to buy pelts from the Indians, thus making a tidy fortune for himself.

At first things went well, but the plan soon backfired. For the Indians, too, made wampum, and they soon returned with their own money and demanded for it such goods as cloth, knives, and guns. Shell money, far too much of it for actual use, began to pile up.

In this dilemma Prince had another bright idea. For good English currency he sold his surplus shell money to distant traders in New York, Pennsylvania, and Canada. With these hard-money profits he opened his bank, and became known as the first banker of Maine.

Some readers may still find it hard to understand just how shells can become money. In this respect shells may be compared to gold. Both are found free in nature for the taking. But both are inaccessible to most people, and work is required to obtain them. Presumably their value derives from their ultimate scarcity. Even today, although Cape Cod is less than two hours from my home, I should have to make a small expedition if I wanted a bushel of quahogs. And I should have to buy them from a shell fisherman who has a license to take them from the water.

The Indians prepared their shell money by making strings of cylindrical beads cut from clams and other shells. (The Indians of the West Coast used Tusk Shells). The purple and blue beads from the quahogs were called *su-kan-hog*. But the colonists shortened things up in New England by calling all shell money wampum.

Actually the names by which such money was called varied widely in different periods, and in different countries. The English in Virginia called it *roanoke,* and so was derived the name of a great American city. The Dutch called it *zeewan.* The name wampum came from the shortening of the words *wampumpeag,* which in the language of the Algonquins meant "strings of white." The French called it *esnoguy.* In this form the name appears in the following passage in the *Voyages* of Jacques Cartier (1535): "The most precious article they [the Hurons] possessed was *esnoguy,* which is as white as snow. They procure it from shells in the river, of which they make a sort of bead which has the same use among them as gold or silver with us. It has the value of stopping nosebleed; for we tried it."

It is especially interesting to note that, while wampum was being used as money in the American continent, it was not used for exchange with the yellow Money Cowry, which was being used at the same time, and had been used for millenniums, as the basic currency of much of the tropical world of other continents. East and West have always been very far apart.

44. FOR THE BIRDS

Shellfish are eaten by us all as something of a delicacy, in the form of an occasional clam chowder, or perhaps a plate of scallops. But for certain birds shellfish are a staple, almost their only diet. You may live in a warm climate or, as warmer weather unlocks the snow, you may be able to get to the beach, with a little time to be idle outdoors. It is an experience in itself to watch the seagulls as they fly over the edge of the ocean, searching and searching in that incessant hunt for food which keeps the wild creation always on the edge of survival.

Everyone who collects shells keeps close watch on the tides, for it is only at dead low that it is very rewarding to examine the beach near the tide mark or to wade in, scouring the bottom for any live mollusk that may be lurking there. But no matter how early you get to the shore, the gulls will get there first and take their pick. For, with all the time there is, they are there before you, and will stay after you have left.

They may even do you the favor of finding a specimen or two, eating the contents, and leaving the cleaned shells behind for you. So the hovering gulls at low tide may be a sign that you will get the very kind of specimens you are looking for.

44. Moon Shells dropped on rock by gulls.

While you are shelling you may find it entertaining to watch the swarming and swooping of the gulls. It takes quite a little detective work to find out exactly what it is that they are eating. Once, just after a hurricane that missed the mainland but battered Cape Cod, I was there at Chatham Beach, Massachusetts, watching the gulls and their special feast of shellfish torn up and cast ashore by the violent waters. As I watched, I could see a gull swoop down, snatch something, and rise with it in its beak. But you can never get really close to gulls on the wing and, try as I would, I could not descry just what the gull was holding in its beak. I determined to stick to it until I could find out.

Time after time a gull would release its hold and drop its prey. Time after time the object fell in a pool of water or was lost so that I could not find it among the distant rocks. Finally I set a bead on one dropped specimen and made a beeline for the spot at the margin of the water. There, sure enough, was the shell of a bay scallop, with only one ring, showing it to be less than a year old. It is against the law to take scallops so young but the gulls are no keepers of the law. All along the beach were small bay scallops, torn open, their two valves agape, cleaned bare of their meat, the fresh bits of muscle still sticking to the valves.

A favorite catch of the gulls along the waterline of Atlantic shores, from the Gulf of St. Lawrence to North Carolina, is the big Moon Shell *Lunatia heros* Say. It looks like a large gray-white, globe-shaped snail. This could be called a gull's favorite. But from a gull's point of view it is a tough specimen to conquer. Often I have seen a gull catch one in his beak at low tide and fly ashore, hovering over a patch of bare, flat rocks. So exact is instinct, or experience, that the gull mounts just the right height for a smash, lets go the shell, and it crashes to its ruin on the rock plateau below.

There is sand on every side, and the rock area is small, so that sometimes the bird misses. If so, it snatches at its prey once more, and is up again until the shell is smashed by a fall. The gull then devours the meat on the spot, or picks out a tender morsel and flies away, leaving the shell remains behind. Like a field of dead men's bones, the broken shells collect and bleach white on the rocks, evidence of many a meal well eaten.

If it is quiet by the sea one may be inclined to meditate on the spectacle. Here a drama that has been played on these shores from the beginning of their time is played before us and will continue being played for what more of time there is. Here is ready-made entertainment for the generations of men who never cease to wander at the edge of the sea.

45. EGG-LAYING SNAILS

Many a youngster and many a grown-up, roaming our sandy beaches, has been thoroughly puzzled to discover fragile collars of sand which have no apparent origin or purpose. Actually, they are the egg cases of one or the other of two Moon Shells which go by several common names, such as Bull's Eye or Shark's Eye. One of these, with a deep umbilicus, is called by the scientific name *Lunatia heros* Say; the other, which has a callus over the umbilicus, is known to scientists as *Polinices duplicatus* Say.

They live in intertidal areas along the beaches of New England. The shells are globe-shaped and of a bluish gray. The interior of the lip is stained with orange-tan and purple. The dark spot on the spire, looking something like an eye, accounts for some of the common names. In their larger sizes they are about 2 to $4\frac{1}{2}$ inches high. These are shells the gulls search for at earliest low tide. Flying high with a captured specimen, they may be seen to drop it on a patch of rock, to feast on its broken remains.

One would hardly suspect that these sand collars are actually the nests or egg cases of these much-sought-after mollusks. The collars provide us with one link in the complex processes by which millions of living mollusks

45. Moon Shells with sand-collar egg cases.

project their species through millenniums of time. The mating behavior of mollusks is complex, and varies widely from species to species. Until recently, moreover, it has been studied only in the most sketchy fashion, and is still wide open as a field of research. Shell collectors have been, for long, chiefly interested in the attractiveness of their collections and their display cabinets. Lately, however, they have become more interested in molluscan behavior. This expansion of interests has been aided by shell clubs in many cities, and by the clubs' mimeographed or printed publications.

These particular shells' efforts to carry on their race are just one example of the many patterns used by various mollusks. The mollusks exhibit practically all forms of reproduction. Even so, we know little of the mating behavior of the Moon Shell, or of marine mollusks in general.

Land snails are reported to have special ways of showing and stimulating affection by circling, touching, and special use of the tentacles. It is thought that marine mollusks show less elaborate procedures. But, in the case of the Moon Shell, it is known that the female lays its eggs in long lines in the gelatinous sand collar shown in plate 45.

Nature is very prodigal in the quantity of young that hatch out, because only a small number can survive to adulthood. Myriads are devoured as food for other creatures, and countless others perish because they do not find food or lodgment. I know of no count of the eggs in the sand collar, but it is reported that the common European mussel spawns five to twelve million eggs.

As the Moon Shell lays its eggs, it exudes a gelatinous substance that holds the sand lightly together. This substance is molded over the shell with eggs embedded in it until it forms the sand collar. As you walk the beach you may see these sand collars at different times or different places, and in different stages of development. By examining them you may find some in which a certain amount of growth has taken place, so that the tiny creatures may be seen in spiral rings of tiny swellings around the sand collar.

The whole structure is extremely fragile, even difficult to pick up. If you wish to examine one it would be well to moisten the sand and move the collar very gently. It is difficult to preserve intact unless sprayed by some protective plastic substance to hold it in place for display.

46. THE ODD BEHAVIOR OF THE SLIPPER SHELLS

An account has been given here of the way in which the Moon Shell carries on its race by depositing its eggs in a sand collar. Along the same eastern shores of the United States, one of this mollusk's close neighbors on the beach, in intertidal waters, is the common Atlantic Slipper Shell, *Crepidula fornicata* L. This mollusk propagates its species in quite an unusual way, exhibiting both an odd way of living and a most remarkable form of sex behavior. This creature is first cousin to the Eastern White Slipper Shell, *Crepidula plana* Say.

The common name Slipper Shell is given to members of the genus *Crepidula* because they are thought to resemble slippers. On the inside, where the foot would go into the slipper, the animal lives, partly under a plaque or shelf that would form the upper part of the slipper. When the creature is removed, the shell looks as if a tiny foot might be inserted. The scientific name of the species, *fornicata,* means "arched," or "vaulted." This name is appropriate because of the shell's habit of piling up, one on the back of another, to form a hump, or arched colony, or because the shell itself is formed as a hump.

The Slipper Shell, running from $\frac{3}{4}$ of an inch to 2 inches in size, is found up and down most of the Atlantic

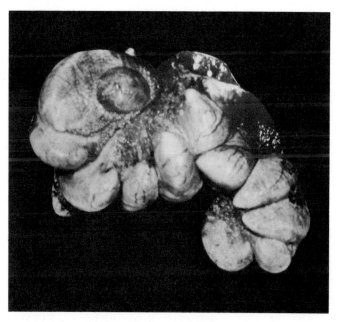

46. Pile-up of Slipper Shells (*Crepidula fornicata* L.).

Coast from Canada to the Gulf of Mexico. It has even been introduced to the West Coast of the United States. If the mollusks live on muddy or sandy bottoms, where there is nothing to fasten their shells to, they attach themselves to one another, and pile up into curling groups or masses. But these piles cannot be simply preserved as they are, because, although they hold tight to one another on the beach, if they are dried or boiled they fall apart.

The reproductive behavior of *Crepidula fornicata* is interesting, even surprising. This mollusk exhibits both sex phasing and sex reversal. During the early part of its life, the Slipper Shell passes through a male phase, and later through a female phase. Hence the males are always much smaller and younger than the females. The young male, which gradually develops a pointed male organ called the verge, or penis, wanders about until it finds one of its species which is in the female phase. Having discovered such a mate, it attaches itself to the dorsal side of the female, adjacent to the female copulatory organs. The female lays its eggs in capsules, brooding over them under her foot until they grow enough to be set free.

The initial act of reproduction having been performed, the individual in the male stage gradually passes into a medial or ambisexual phase. The verge shrinks and disappears, being succeeded by female organs. The animal, which in its male phase wandered about in typical male fashion, now settles down and remains relatively stationary, waiting for a young male to arrive to initiate a new brood. This phenomenal sex reversal, unusual in nature, endows the humble Slipper Shell with a uniqueness which makes it worthy of any shell collection.

47. ODD PLACES
TO FIND SHELLS

To the lay individual the finding of seashells may be associated with the tidelines and walks along the beach. Actually, relatively few shells of considerable worth are found in this way, except after a big storm. When the ocean has been deeply agitated by strong winds, much sea life is torn away from its natural place in the deeps and is cast up on the shore. Even after such a disturbance, however, you will have to have stamina to get there early, before other collectors who watch weather and tides.

Even along the shore, the tide pools must be carefully looked into. Rocks must be turned over, and seaweed masses of material cast up by the waves meticulously examined. The large shell in plate 47 was picked up by my wife at Chatham, on Cape Cod. It is a specimen of the Channeled Whelk, *Busycon canaliculatum* L., a beautifully sculptured shell when taken alive. This one, however, is very dead indeed, and much battered. It is worthwhile because of its encrustation of smaller shells.

These little shells are specimens of the small, very attractive Eastern White Slipper Shell, *Crepidula plana* Say, common all the way from Canada through the eastern United States into Florida and the West Indies. They range from $\frac{1}{2}$ inch to $1\frac{1}{2}$ inches in length and are milky white, flat, and possibly slightly concave or convex. They

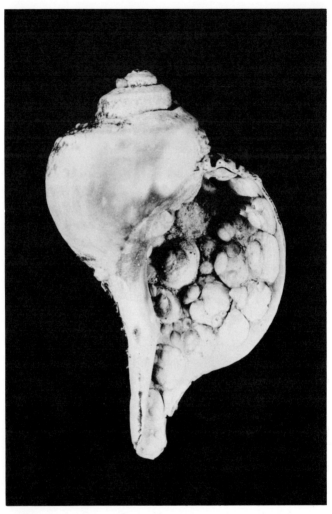

47. Eastern White Slipper Shell (*Crepidula plana* Say), growing on a dead *Busycon canaliculatum* L.

adhere to whatever hard surface they can obtain, practically always that of a dead shell. In this case, they fastened themselves to the inside surface of the lip of a large whelk.

To discover these shells one should peer into some broken-down debris which might otherwise not be worth looking at. The little shells are a bit fragile, but they can be removed easily by boiling them briefly, along with the shell to which they are attached.

Another odd place to look for encrusted shells is on navigation buoys. The malacologist Dr. Arthur Merrill made a special study of these buoys, and reported his findings in *Remarks Concerning the Benefits of Systematic and Repetitive Collecting from Navigation Buoys* (1950).

The account is helpful for any of us who want to follow in the writer's pattern. He points out that, when buoys are brought in for periodic cleaning and servicing by the Coast Guard, they are likely to be covered with quite a few species of marine life, so getting to them before they are cleaned up may be rewarding. It would be hard to say what species will be encountered, since this would vary from place to place. Each buoy presents its own complex community, a totality of related parts. It is possible that among the shells found would be mussels, some of the jingle shells, chitons, and limpets.

Shell collectors learn to keep their eyes open in all directions, and to look over anything related to the sea. It is common practice to study the pillars of old wharves, and their underspaces, at low tide. One collector got permission to stand by the fish chute on which the leftovers of cleaned fish were carried out. Examining the stomachs, she obtained some interesting shells *ex pisce*.

48. SHELLCRAFT

An astonishing number of people make a hobby of shell-craft, the art of combining seashells in an endless series of patterns for ornamentation and decoration. Some of these products are fashioned into souvenirs at such coastal cities as Saint Petersburg, Florida. They are sold in vast numbers to tourists, and present a very wide range of taste.

Shellcraft ornaments are made in homes by workers who conduct something like a cottage industry, hoping to sell their earrings, plaques, and ash trays to local distributors such as gift shops. Many carry on shellcraft just for the fun of it, using their hobby as an outlet for their decorative or creative urges.

Shellcraft is used also by schoolteachers in programs which require handwork, and by camp counselors, who find that shells have an outdoor, natural significance very appropriate for a camp program. Some therapists have found shellcraft very helpful in their work with handicapped persons and with convalescents.

Beginners in shellcraft usually work, at first, with some set of simple examples or patterns prepared by others. To do so they usually turn to books of explanation and direction, the best form of aid in this kind of work. One of the simplest books for this purpose is *Shell Art,* by Helen K. Krauss (1965).

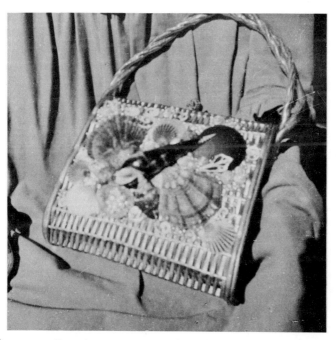

48. Handbag, by Mrs. A. E. Adair of Hawaii.

The photograph of a decorated handbag in plate 48 was sent to me by a very skillful shellcrafter, Mrs. A. E. Adair of Honolulu. She makes lovely ornamental plaques and cleverly decorated baskets for herself and for some of her friends. Of her work Mrs. Adair said, in a letter to me: "In doing natural-color wall plaques, plastic boxes, and so on, and in all gold spray work, I use lots of dried sea-weed. But for the finer type of decoration only the small delicate varieties of shells are useful."

The handbag in plate 48 should encourage anyone who is interested in shellcraft as a personal hobby, as it shows a fine pattern for an object both good-looking and useful. The selection of shells used on this particular handbag is delightful and different. The large black conical shell at center makes the composition unusual, and, with their diverging ribs, the scallops prove excellent for pattern and color.

For some shell enthusiasts such work with shells is anathema. This may be because of the debased and vulgar taste displayed in much of the rubble sold to tourists at some seaside resorts. It is heartbreaking to pass the stalls in Acapulco and see crooked, ill-made lamps and bastard ornaments made from lovely shells like the Queen Conch and the yellow Lamp Shell, *Xancus angulatus* Solander. On the other hand the discriminating observer will some-times see a framed shell "picture," or a really artistic bit of shellcraft. Should we not be liberal enough to make proper distinctions and not deny appreciation to those who have genuine artistry?

49. SHELLS FOR
INTERIOR DECORATION

The Japanese, perhaps the most beauty-sensitive of all peoples, customarily set aside in a room a clear space in which to display some work of art or object of natural beauty which is changed from time to time. The background space areas of modern architecture suggest a similar treatment for Western-style homes. An excellent decorative effect may be secured by an arrangement of seashells. A single colorful shell from distant seas may provide adequate interest, or any group of shells set up for contrasting form or color.

Unlike flowers, which fade all too soon, seashells remain as a relatively permanent decoration. So they are finding increasing favor with both amateur and professional decorators. This trend is furthered by color photographs in favorite home magazines of seashells used in table and shelf decoration.

I know one friend who has five or six carefully chosen shells in a round glass bowl making up a centerpiece used on his rather grand dinner table. Another gentleman had my wife design for him a shelf for about twenty-five specially chosen shells. She designed it in three half-moon mirrors, each larger than the other toward the bottom, and separated by clear plastic pillars. It adorned his

49. Decorative Grouping.

mansion on the Hudson, the shells reflecting their beauty down deep in a well of light.

Inquiries come in frequently concerning some aspect of the use of shells in home beautification. Such inquiries are very difficult to answer, and up to now there has been no book on this complex subject, and no extensive treatment of it. These few paragraphs can barely open up the matter but still may be useful.

Plate 49 shows how simply such a decoration can be made. It is composed of four beautiful but very different shells. The back-piece is a split specimen of the Nautilus standing on a Chinese teakwood rack. To the left is a specimen of the Giant Venus Comb, *Murex troscheli* Lischke; the large shell is a specimen of the Branched *Murex, Murex ramosus*. The smooth shell, a pure white Egg Shell, *Ovula ovum,* gives a perfect contrast in form.

But this grouping is a mere example. Each person may choose and group his own shells. With ten or twelve carefully made selections it is possible to arrange quite a series of "bouquets."

Shells make magnificent window decorations in a shop or home. They may be set up in cabinets or on shelves and may be changed, rearranged, or added to for pleasing effect. A shiny surface, a mirror base, or a pottery bowl all provide good background.

That all-time favorite, the Chambered Nautilus, can be set up as a vase with four tiny shells like "button shells" cemented on as a stand. Such a natural base is usually more attractive than an artificial base. The whole shell may be attractively flanked by the two halves of a split specimen, showing the inner chambers.

Color is best introduced by setting an orange-colored Japanese Noble Scallop, *Pecten nobilis,* beside a purple one. The red-mouthed Cameo Shell, *Cassis rufa,* from East Africa, is an inexpensive shell which gives a spot of color in a specimen of fair size.

A large, fine shell that can be used to center a group and also to hold flowers, on occasion, is the Australian Melon Shell; the large Imperial Volute, *Voluta imperialis* can also be used in this way, as can the unusual Angled Volute, once *Voluta angulata,* now *Voluta dufresnei,* from Uruguay. Famous and unique is the Triton Shell, *Charonia tritonis,* often from the Fiji Islands.

Among the general favorites admired for form or color are the large scallops, *Pecten magellanicus* and *Pecten yessoensis;* the superb Wonder Shell, *Thatcheria mirabilis;* and the black-and-white Marble Cone, *Conus marmoreus.* A number of less expensive decorative shells are the Tiger Cowry, *Cypraea tigris;* the Mourning Cowry, *Cypraea mauritiana;* and the Blue Abalone, *Haliotis fulgens,* which is like a bowl of iridescent blue and green.

Those who can afford distinction and who, in course of time, care to add a *pièce de résistance,* may well look forward to owning an aristocratic shell like the Emperor's Top, *Perotrochus hirasei,* or the Courtly Volute, *Voluta aulica.* For these there are always requests from sophisticated collectors, because these shells are both rare and very attractive.

50. SEASHELLS IN
A CONTEMPORARY
ARTIST'S WORK

Seashells appear in a number of remarkable paintings by Ethlyn Woodlock, in recent years a frequent exhibitor in some of the country's most important galleries. As the reproduction here so clearly shows, Mrs. Woodlock's highly imaginative treatment of her subject creates an illusion of reality, and at the same time evokes a certain higher reality.

The oil painting in plate 50 is called *Ole Beachcomber, M.D.* It can hardly be better described than in Mrs. Woodlock's own words, as follows:

> On the wall of a shack,
> By the side of the sea,
> Hangs a "Doctor IN" sign,
> Of a retired M.D.
>
> . . .
>
> Reminiscent of boyhood,
> And unmindful of the weather,
> Are bird's egg and skull,
> Old marbles and feather.
>
> . . .
>
> Crab case, and the lucky
> Half of a chicken wishbone.

50. Ole Beachcomber, M.D. Courtesy of Ethelyn Woodlock.

A claw pinches his watch,
As he is alone with—

TIME for fishing,
TIME for reminiscing,
TIME to find a conch
With spiral interior,
Or a wing shell, nacre on nacre,
Building real pearl superior.

TIME for thinking of the Sea,
Lifetime study of
Ole Beachcomber, M.D.

Mrs. Woodlock, an ardent shell collector, lives in Midland Park, New Jersey, in a charming old house which is virtually an art gallery of her paintings.

Because of the masterful, polished realism of her style, Mrs. Woodlock is much sought after as a portraitist. Yet her finest work is of the type shown here, in a style which could be called "super-realism." Although it is related to Dali's early style, it is free of Dali's sensationalism. Many of her paintings, like the one shown in plate 50, have a quiet intimacy, a homely, prankish, personal appeal rarely seen. In most of them you will find, somewhere in the picture, a seashell.

51. SHELLS ON
POSTAGE STAMPS

Brightly colored and beautifully designed postage stamps add to the simple daily pleasures of those who exchange seashells with collectors in far countries. Hummingbirds, tropical orchids, exotic fruits, goldfish, and magnificent wild animals brighten up some of the stamps that come in, especially if they arrive from Oriental countries. But seldom is a stamp frankly taken over by a seashell.

Yet that has recently happened. Some seashell collectors have been receiving, on their mail from Japan, a fascinating stamp featuring that country's most famous seashell, the Emperor's Top, *Perotrochus hirasei* Pilsbry. The background of the stamp is a dark coffee-brown, suitable to show off the gracefully sloping form of the shell, its pointed spire, and its famous slit running out from the opening. The bright red waved markings show clearly against the white of the shell, giving the whole stamp a very smart and unusual appearance.

The use of this shell to adorn a stamp was a particularly happy choice by the Japanese Post Office. Few shells from any part of the world are more graceful. And this one is probably more clearly identified with Japan, in the thoughts of shell collectors, than any other shell.

It is reported that once every specimen found was

51. Postage stamp showing Emperor's Top Shell (*Perotrochus hirasei* Pilsbry).

given as a gift to the Emperor. Presumably this is the origin of the common name, the Emperor's Top. It does look very much like a top, the kind that is spun in almost every country of the world, including Japan. This shell is fairly large, an adult specimen being about four inches across the base.

It comes from deep water and is, of course, rare. For centuries it has been much prized by collectors, just as it is now by everyone fortunate enough to own one.

There are other shell stamps. From the Maldive Islands in the Indian Ocean, southwest of India, a letter came to me several years ago bearing just one five-laree stamp depicting a collection of shells that I cannot identify from the picture. The whole is a graceful grouping showing one large Helmet Shell in the background and a cowry, bottom forward in front of the lot. The grouping of orange-brown shells is set at center on a white background and the whole is framed by a fretwork design, also shown in orange-brown against white. This shell stamp is the only one that has actually come on a letter addressed to me. I have not been able to secure more as gifts to other shell collectors.

A number of shell stamps I have never yet seen, except in pictures. Some of them are illustrations for a recent book, *Universal Shells* (1961). These illustrations appear near the end, just before the index. Unfortunately the author, Maxwell Smith, who distributed his own shell books, died shortly after the book was published, so that it seems to have become unavailable.

Among the stamps illustrated in *Universal Shells* is a 1914 stamp of the German Reich showing *Nautilus pom-*

pilus, the Chambered Nautilus of Dresden. Another pictured is a Paper Nautilus, *Argonauta argo,* on a 1956 stamp of Jugoslavia.

Issued by the Ryukyu Islands, in 1948 and 1960 respectively, are a stamp showing a Helmet Shell, and one with a Lambis Shell set in a grouping. A *Murex* appears with some others on a stamp from French Polynesia dated 1959. A small *Strombus* in the corner below a picture of Queen Victoria came from the Bahamas in 1882, and a similar stamp, with the shell shown below Queen Elizabeth, appeared in 1949. There is also a sixpenny Cayman Island stamp on which a picture of the Queen appears with a picture of a seashell. Finally, I note the painted Snail *Polymita picta* Born, on a stamp from Oriente Province, Cuba.

Doubtless there are other shell stamps which have not reached my attention. A few are listed by my friend, Tom Rice, in an article that appeared in a Pacific Northwest shell club publication a few years ago.

A new and beautiful series of stamps picturing seashells has been issued in Papua and New Guinea. Designed by the Australian artist Paul Jones, they are printed in four-color rotogravure by Helio Courvosier of Switzerland. Information concerning these may be obtained by writing the Philatelic Bureau, Department of Post and Telegraphs, Port Moresby, Papua and New Guinea.

52. THE POTTERY SNAILS
OF TONALA

Occasionally one comes across art objects which portray or represent snails. The pottery-ware snails from Mexico shown in plate 52 are both naturalistic and artistic in their design and would be suitable adornments for the home of any admirer of shells. Their naturalism may be checked by looking at the two Cuernavaca snails in plate 22.

The ornamental snails have an attractive touch in the graceful decorations of deep blue and red-brown. The sides of the snails are enhanced by appropriate small spirals, and the back has a lovely petaled flower with a spiral center set against leafy patterns. It was with considerable surprise that I discovered these beautiful little ceramic snails in the tourist town of Tlaquepaque.

Tlaquepaque is a suburb of Guadalajara in west-central Mexico. It is a center for the display of Mexican arts, perhaps the most remarkable to be found anywhere in that country. Indeed Tlaquepaque is something of a dream world for those who admire beautiful things in leather, fabrics, glass, pottery, or silver. One of the main streets is lined with grand emporia which resemble museums. In them a traveler can wander undisturbedly by the hour. In many parts of Mexico, tawdry wares in vulgar taste are sold to unsophisticated tourists. But on this avenue in Tlaquepaque artistic standards are high.

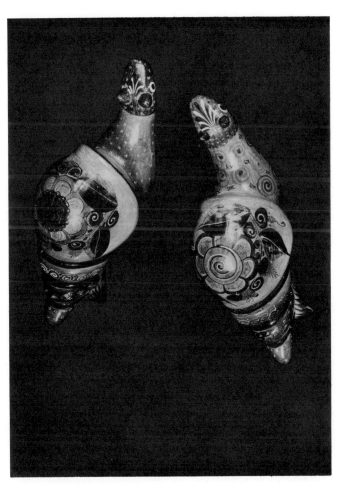

52. Lovely Tonala Snails.

The real source of the ceramic marvels on sale in the shops of Tlaquepaque is the nearby town of Tonala. There I found the patterned snails lying on the floor and shelves of a fascinating factory inside a modest doorway on a side street. Here, in a veritable zoo of small and larger pottery animals, I also found a gray armadillo, decorated playfully with yellow and white daisies, as well as huge and tiny turtles with motile heads and tails.

There was one other type of large ceramic snail, a perfect globose model. It, too, had its motile head. In this riot of charming design and color, choosing was most difficult. But in the end I left with a small private zoo of my own, including two pairs of snails.

The presence of these beautiful pieces of pottery, and of other modern works of art, is due to something of an artistic renaissance in the appearance of what is known as the "Tonala School." In the previous two decades something of a decline in taste, such as usually follows mass tourism in a country, had occurred in Mexican arts and crafts. But one's faith in the eternal vitality of art is renewed by the story of Tonala. It all emerged from the work of Jorge Wilmott, a native of Monterrey, Mexico, who organized a cooperative workshop about a decade ago among the artisans of Tonala. Under his sure direction a new series of thoroughly original, hand-decorated art objects of superb beauty is proceeding from Tonala's workshops and kilns. What has taken place there must rate as one of the most vital artistic developments taking place anywhere in the world in the past decade. I am grateful to the workers concerned for my little zoo of snails and such.

53. THE JENNY HANIVER

When you wander about the ports of the world looking for shells you are sure to find some novelty of the sea you have not seen before. On several visits to Veracruz, Mexico, I have found only a few shells. But on the very first trip my wife and I made to that active port some years ago, we ran across an interesting curiosity of the sea.

There in a small store window was a bottle filled with some dark liquid in which was preserved what was marked as a Pez Diablo, or Devil Fish. Some years later I got the photograph you see here (plate 53), which makes it amply clear just why it was given the name Devil Fish.

At first I had no idea what this strange creature might be. As time went on, however, the mystery began to unfold. Gradually I discovered that it was something of a fabrication. The fish used is a species of ray. Parts of the fish are cut away, the head and mouth distorted, the fins removed, and the fleshy parts raised up to form wings. Other parts are set in place to suit the designer, and the whole is then dried flat in its fantastic form. Little by little I learned more about these specimens. In old natural history books they are called by various names such as Dragons, Basilisks, and Jenny Hanivers.

It seems that the first known illustration of a Jenny

53. The Jenny Haniver.

Haniver was in a Latin work called *De Piscium Et Aquatilium Animantium Natura,* published in Zurich, Switzerland, in 1558. A translation of part of the text tells us that quack medicine vendors and others of that ilk dry the rays and fashion them in various and wonderful shapes. A volume titled *De Piscibus,* published in Bologna, Italy, in 1613 shows men fashioning rays into diverse shapes to be used by vendors or performers to attract the attention of the populace.

Thus it becomes clear that these so-called Devil Fish, though still sufficiently rare to be curious, are by no means a modern phenomenon. They are said to have been fairly common in private European museums of the 17th and 18th centuries. Some of these fantastically formed fish were fabricated out of sharks. Devil Fish were made in considerable numbers in Italy in the 16th century.

It is reported that Jenny Hanivers sometimes are found in nature. By a freak, the pectoral fins of some of the rays fail to grow fast to the sides of the head and remain in a floating condition.

Recently I was walking one evening among the lighted stalls along the Malecon in Acapulco, Mexico. To my surprise I saw some small ten-inch Jenny Hanivers hanging for sale among the mixed merchandise of the small street-side shops. I picked up about a dozen of these Devil Fish for a few pesos each and brought them back with me to the United States. In all probability Jenny Hanivers still will be found by anyone who wants to look for them on the streets or in the markets of Acapulco.

54. GOOSE BARNACLES

The word *shell* is not exactly the same as the word *mollusk*. Crabs, which are crustaceans, have shells. The Pacific Goose Barnacle, *Mitella polymerus,* and the Acorn Barnacle, *Balanus glandula* of California, have shells but, being crustaceans, they are less related to the mollusks than they are to crabs and shrimps. Some of these barnacles are edible and are to be bought in the markets in Mexico City where they are sold as food.

A shell collector is to be pardoned if he does not notice that a barnacle is not a mollusk. Early authorities on shells did not make any such distinction. Donovan, in his *British Sea Shells* (1799) has a vivid picturing of what he calls the Anatiferous Acorn Shell, which he identifies as *Lepas anatifera.* He says:

> *Lepas anatifera* is found on the coasts of England and Ireland but more frequently on that of Scotland. It adheres by means of branches, or pedicles, to the bottom of ships, planks, logs, and other substances floating in water.
>
> This curious marine production consists of many unequal membraneous branches, or arms, at the ends of which the shells are disposed in an irregular man-

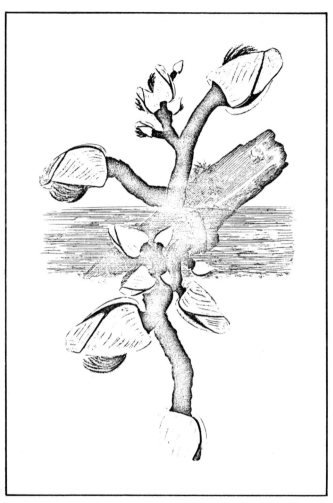

54. Goose Barnacles.

ner, the larger clustering with the smaller in groups, and forming bunches of various sizes. The branches are of fine red, the shells of bluish violet. The animal within is a *triton,* and is furnished with many *cirrhi,* or *tentacula,* curling, slender appendages with which it takes its food. These *tentacula* are pectinated like feathers, and hang out of the shells when open.

Donovan continues his account by quoting further from an antique manuscript which he refers to as *Gerard's Herbal.* He gives it in the orginal spelling as follows:

What our eyes have seene, and hands have touched, we shall declare. There is a small island in Lancashire, called the Pile of Foulders, wherein are found the broken pieces of old and bruised ships, some whereof have been cast thither by shipwrake, and also the trunks and bodies with the branches of old and rotten trees, cast up there likewise; whereon is found a certain spume, or froth, that in time breedeth unto certaine shels, in shape like those of a muskle, but sharper pointed and of a whitish color, wherein is contained a thing in form like a lace of silke finely woven, as it were, together, of a whitish colour; one end whereof is fastened unto the inside of the shell, even as the fish of oisters and muskles are: the other end is made fast unto the belly of a rude masse, or lumpe, which in time cometh to the shape and form of a bird. When it is perfectly formed, the shell gapeth open, and the first thing that appeareth is the foresaid lace or string, next come the legs of the bird, hanging out, and as it groweth greater it openeth the shel by degrees, till at langthe it is all come forth, and hangeth only by the bill: in short space after it cometh to full maturities, and falleth into the sea, where it gathereth feathers, and groweth to fowle bigger than a Mallard and lesser than a goose, having black legs and bill or beake, and feathers blacke and white, spotted in such a manner as is our Magpie, called in some places a Pie-Annet, which the people of Lancashire, call by no other name than a *tree Goose*: which place aforesaid, and all these parts adjoyning, do so much abound therewith, if any doubt, may it please them to repair unto me, and I shall satisfie by the testimonie of good witnesses.

ON THE TRAIL—
INDOORS
AND OUTDOORS

55. CAPE COD
NATIONAL SEASHORE

Cape Cod is one of the leading holiday resorts of the United States, a bit of Massachusetts that juts right out into the sea. Because of this, it has vast stretches of shoreline in easy reach and is relatively cool in summer. It is a Mecca for summer visitors and a favorite spot for sea-boating of all kinds.

So varied and complete are the facilities and resources of this remarkable public park that no one should miss an opportunity to visit it when it is open, during the summer months. The glassed-in Visitor Center (plate 55) is full of interesting exhibits, including some seashells, for Cape Cod is also a good place for shelling, and beachcombing is a prime entertainment there.

Long stretches of the Cape's East Coast, from Nauset Beach to Wellfleet and beyond, face the open sea. Here are immense sweeps of sandy beach. But sandy beaches are usually unrewarding places for shelling, except at very low tide. And at low tide the gulls usually get there first.

Luck is likely to be much better on the more protected beaches about Pleasant Bay, from East Orleans to Chatham, and around the corner of the Cape to the section protected by Monomoy Island near South Chatham. Living mollusks are sometimes found here, especially at

55. Visitor Center at Eastham, Massachusetts.

low tide. It is not unusual to find the humpbacked piles of the Canoe Shell, *Crepidula fornicata* L, and the smaller *Crepidula plana* Say, called the Slipper Shell. Sometimes a specimen of one of the larger Pear Fulgars, *Busycon canaliculatum* L, is found near water's edge at lowest tide. This must be taken home and boiled about twenty minutes. Then the operculum may be pried off easily with a knife, and a fork may be inserted in the large fleshy foot. By rolling the flesh around and about the shell you may easily remove the whole animal. Its spiral form and varied color are wonders to behold.

Many a recently dead shell may be picked up at high-water mark, where the receding tides have left a line of miscellaneous debris, seaweed, bits of wood, and broken shells. Here is usually found the Surf Clam, *Spisula solidissima* Dillwyn, the Jingle Shell, *Anomia simplex* Orb., and the False Angel Wing, *Petricola pholadiformis* Lam. There are plenty of mussels, *Mytilis edulis* L., and a smattering of Razor Clams, *Ensis directus* Conrad. These may be picked up dead, but at most beaches a license is required to take live shellfish, as there are no more than enough for local property owners, and there is an important shellfish industry along these shores. A glimpse of this shellfish industry in operation may be seen in a number of places on the South Coast. At the water's edge are a number of huts where fishermen are at work opening their catch of quahog clams.

Others may be fishing their oyster beds close to shore. After October 1, the season begins for the succulent Bay Scallop, *Pecten irradians* Lam. If you are so inclined, you may buy whatever is in season for home consumption.

In any case, near the huts are piles of the discarded shells of all of the above, and you may freely take your pick. Thus, even if you did not catch anything yourself, you need not return empty-handed. When you get home you may further amuse yourself by looking up your specimens, if you are fortunate enough to have a copy of the Golden Press edition of R. Tucker Abbott's *Sea Shells of North America* (1968), in which are found descriptions of all the shells mentioned in this brief account of shelling on Cape Cod.

If you take the time to explore Cape Cod still further, you will find at the Visitor Center guidance as to what you may see, what you can do, and where you may go in the wide stretches of this beautiful place.

According to your tastes you may drive around a bit, or park your car and wander on the sand at water's edge, or swim at the appointed place. To be more strenuous you may take walking or bicycling trips, which are full of interest.

For certain special activities, which take place on different days, reservations must be made, but they afford fine privileges. They include a Tidal Marsh trip, a five-hour jaunt to Great Island, and a five-hour trip through the dunes and tidal flats of Hatches Harbor. Also, a very special opportunity for those artistically inclined is a combination sketching and interpretive trip, led by a trained art teacher. No art training or skill is required, although it is of course useful to have some.

For other special activities you should consult the Salt Pond Visitor Center, at Eastham. It has a guided bicycle tour, on your own bicycle, and a Sunset Beach walk (on special dates only). This is an evening walk along the beach, with a campfire after sunset, and a return trip by moonlight.

For all these activities, and those mentioned in the following paragraphs, there is no charge. One may park without cost by the Vistor Center, but a parking permit for all five beaches, for the day, costs a dollar.

Because of the freedom they afford, perhaps the most interesting of all the special activities are the self-guided trails, and the bicycle trails, for which you need make no reservations, and on which you may follow your own timing. Take whichever you prefer of five well-marked walking trails: at Province Lands, the Province Lands Nature Trail; at North Truro, the Small's Swamp Nature Trail, and Pilgrim Spring History Trail; at Eastham, the Red Maple Swamp Nature Trail; and, at Salt Pond, the Nauset Marsh Nature Trail. Bicycle trails start at Beach Forest Parking area, at Pilgrim Heights, and at Eastham.

In addition to daytime events, there is an intriguing program of evening events at Salt Pond Amphitheater, next to the Visitor Center at Eastham. Each evening, including Sunday, at 8:30 P.M. (in fine weather only) there is a special program. Some recent programs included a showing of a film titled *Whaling,* and another called *Exploring Old Cape Cod.*

It is obvious that, to take full advantage of the privileges of Cape Cod National Seashore, one should be equipped with advance information. This may be obtained by writing to the United States Department of the Interior, Bureau of Outdoor Recreation, 128 N. Broad Street, Philadelphia, Pa. Unfortunately the Visitor Center is sometimes out of the needed printed material for the guidance of visitors.

A map is essential to get a picture of the over-all geography in advance. If you arrive on Cape Cod without a map, try to pick up locally a copy of the *Cape Codder Summer Magazine,* which will probably provide you with a map of the Park, and a complete list of current activities.

I should like to ask here for an extensive exhibit, at the Visitor Center, of the shells of Cape Cod. As the shells disappear before the influx of humans, a permanent record of the seashell life on primitive Cape Cod would be worth preserving. Maybe if readers of this book ask for it, an exhibit of this kind can be mounted at the Visitor's Center.

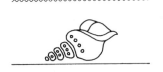

56. VISITING
WOODS HOLE AQUARIUM

Summer is the best time to visit the Aquarium of the Marine Biological Laboratory of Woods Hole, on Cape Cod, Massachusetts. The MBL, as it is called locally, is a project of the federal government, and is one of the most famed centers of marine biology to be found anywhere in the world.

Situated on the landmost tip of Cape Cod, where it juts out between Buzzards Bay and Nantucket Sound, the town of Woods Hole has become a magic name for all those interested in mollusks and all the denizens of the sea. The research carried on there occupies a number of buildings and makes use of a small fleet of working ships.

To aid in its ever expanding and highly important studies, the MBL has recently acquired a laboratory ship, the *Albatross*. It is a vessel specially built for its purpose. On a tour of the *Albatross* I was able to inspect with awe its fine equipment and special machinery installed for deep-sea dredging.

By means of a windlass and nylon cables, a specially constructed dredge or basket may be lowered to the deep bottom. As the basket scrapes the bottom, a load of muddy, mixed materials is secured, lifted by the winches, and deposited on the deck. The materials are then ex-

56. The *Albatross*.

amined and searched to see what has been the luck of the operation. Each expedition is commissioned to secure material needed for scientific work under way, ranging from the dissection of a particular mollusk to a study of the effect of tranquilizers on a colony of *tunicata*.

The interior of the ship is set up with magnificently equipped marine laboratories. When the deck material has been sorted, what has been salvaged may be processed, prepared, or studied in the floating laboratories while the ship is still at sea, and the success of the particular trip so determined. The total useful material is returned to the main laboratories at Woods Hole, stored, or placed in tanks of running seawater. Thus it can be kept alive, or shipped out to meet requests for material required by scientists, perhaps in very distant parts.

The MBL is equipped to send out to research scientists some eight hundred various specimens of mollusks, fish, crustaceans, algae, and other material from the sea, delivering to research scientists reasonable amounts of botanical and biological materials needed for worthwhile projects. Requests are received daily. Some of the material sent out includes squid, starfish, sting rays, sea spiders, purple sea-urchins, sand sharks, seapork, lobsters, clams, codfish, and many types of sea growths such as seaweeds from shore or shallow.

A tremendous increase in scientific research and study in the field of marine biology in recent years has been due to increased realization of the importance of the sea and its products. One of the most significant studies under way for some time has been conducted and reported by Dr. Arthur Merrill of the MBL staff, on edible sea-scallops

(*Pecten magellanicus* Gmel). Atlantic deep-sea scallops are dredged at sea by scallop fishermen who sail to the scallop beds in the waters off Cape Cod and New Bedford. Since scallops form a very important commercial crop of a much prized delicacy, a program of conservation is needed so that the crop can be gathered in the most economical fashion. To accomplish this, growth studies have been made by dredging scallops, marking their shells with size and date, returning them to the sea, and studying and measuring any that happen to be re-dredged in later years. Thus the optimum size for the fishing rings of the dragnet is determined.

One of the features of the Aquarium, a prime tourist attraction, is a series of scallop shells mounted and on view. It is astonishing to see the variations in size and in lovely color to be found by selecting a series of shells and arranging them to display their special beauty. And aside from these special features, the Aquarium itself is well worth a visit. In the tanks of running water may be seen some of the fascinating creatures of the sea. Fish, crayfish, mollusks are visible, crawling, lumbering, or darting about the tanks. Whether for study or amusement, here is a fascinating day's outing for a lone tourist or a family.

The Aquarium is easily reached. Just before Sagamore Bridge, over Cape Cod Canal, a right turn and about half an hour's drive carries you direct to the Aquarium on the point, at the edge of the sea. The Aquarium is open to the public every day from 10 A.M. to 5 P.M. during the summer season, July 4 to Labor Day. In these two months it clocks up plenty of visitors during Cape Cod's short, bustling summer boom.

57. CLAMS FOR THE DIGGING

The United States is a clam country, and clam digging might be rated as a minor sport. The favorite coasts for clam digging are the Atlantic coastal beaches of New England and the magnificent stretch of Pacific coast in the state of Washington. One of the earliest persons to gloat in writing over the clam crop was the English adventurer and founder of Virginia, Captain John Smith. In 1616 he wrote, "You shall scarce find any bay, or shallow shore, or cove of sand, where you may not take many clampes, or lobster, or both, at your pleasure." Indeed there are documented records which show that there were times when early settlers who had arrived on the American East Coast in the late fall, finding it was too late for a summer crop, ate clams as a main part of the scanty diet that kept them alive until spring.

In these days, during the summer months, clams are the prey of myriads of seashore holiday seekers who, armed with merely a stick, or with a shovel and pail, haunt the shores at low tide. They are looking for a free meal in the form of clams for clam chowder, or even enough for that evening social event known as a "clam bake." But the East Coast diggers are not after the famous Quahog, or Hard-shell Clam, *Venus mercenaria* L., which does not

57. Washington State clam diggers.
Courtesy of Washington Department of Commerce.

burrow, but is taken by means of a rake. They scour the sandy beaches at dead low tide looking, instead, for the telltale holes left by the soft-fleshed clam of the oval white shell, *Mya arenaria* L. As one walks along the beach, shaking the sand with heavy tread, the giveaway signal comes in the form of a tiny jet of water shot upward as the clam is disturbed. Closing the two valves of the shell, it expels a spurt of water through its extended neck, which is then quickly withdrawn, leaving a visible hole.

Digging with any deliberate or improvised instrument is simple. A shovel soon lays bare a pile of sand in which the white clam shells show through. Half an hour should secure about fifty, enough to drop in hot water for a tasty meal. In about ten minutes all the shells have opened, and are ready for the plate. The whole clams, removed one by one with the fingers and dipped in melted butter, make a gourmet's feast. It is maintained by some that in these days of water pollution, shellfish should not be eaten raw. There are well-authenticated reports going back for generations of minor poisoning and digestive distubances that followed the eating of raw shellfish. Modern studies seem to indicate that at certain times of the year poisonous plankton are consumed by some shellfish, and it is thought that human upsets are caused by eating such shellfish raw.

Visitors to Cape Cod, and to some restricted East Coast areas, may not take any shellfish without a local license. On the West Coast, up to now, Washington State is more hospitable. Most of the Washington beaches, from the Columbia River north to Quinault, are open for clam digging, unless otherwise posted, although the beaches at

Quinault Indian Reservation are closed to non-Indians.

Among the choice, open beaches are Long Beach, the Tokeland-Grayland and Westport areas, reached off Highway 101 south of Gray's Harbor, and all of the North Pacific beaches of Oyhut, Ocean City, Pacific Beach, and Moclips, also on Highway 101.

Here the succulent Razor Clam is the quarry. The clam raider uses a "Clam Gun," which is not a gun but a slender shovel with a short handle. The Razor Clam season runs through September 15, but the best clam tides begin about the first of May, and continue on alternate weeks throughout the summer. The minus tide at first comes at early dawn, but near the weekends clam-digging tides come at the more convenient hours of 7 to 11 A.M.

Spotting the characteristic small holes in the sand, the hunter rapidly scoops out two shovelfuls of sand toward the seaward side. He then kneels, plunges his hand into the hole, and grabs the shell or the neck of the long, razor-shaped creature which is, by now, frantically using its **Y**-shaped digger to escape straight down. The hunter holds on tenaciously for a minute of two, until he breaks the clam's "spirit or suction," pulls him out, and adds him to the growing crop in sack or bucket. This crop may increase until the prescribed limit of eighteen a day has been reached.

58. COLLECTING AT HALIBUT POINT

It would be hard to devise a more pleasant one-day holiday for shell collectors than a visit to Halibut Point Reservation, north of Boston, Massachusetts. This is a spot at which you can hardly miss gathering a number of interesting local specimens. At the same time you will be viewing one of the most picturesque seascapes in the country at a spot which seems utterly remote, but is of easy access. Halibut Point on Cape Ann, near Pigeon Cove, is plainly marked on AAA maps.

It is best approached by turning off Route 128 on to 127, passing Annisquam and Lanesville, and then watching near the top of a slope for a left turn. Running the car in just as far as it will go, you will find a parking place. The ten-minute walk down the footpath is a delightful bit of natural wild. The sea looms ahead in a vast panorama across a bold extrusion of granite rock, almost as dramatic as Nova Scotia's famed Peggy's Cove.

On our last visit my wife and I chose a perfect seventy-five degree day, with the sun shining on an almost windless sea. Fishing boats and other vessels sailed off in the distance. But the vast expanse of rugged rock was completely deserted, pitching down in quarries and rock pools to tangles of seaweed at the water.

258

58. Seascape at Halibut Point.

On a fine spring or fall day this spot is a collector's delight. All you need is a knife for prying, a few cups or paper bags, a pail, and sneakers, for the rocks are slippery and sharp. One should be prepared to get a bit wet, lying prone on damp patches, or wading in tempting shallows.

Periwinkles, *Littorina littorea* L., are plentiful, and because it is a clean shore they should be fit to boil and eat at home. Americans tend to neglect these tasty morsels, which are so much prized as tidbits in England and other European countries. The Atlantic Dog Whelk, *Thais lapillus* L., is so plentiful in shallow triangles of water that you may select the beauties, colored, patched, or striped, and leave the ordinary white ones behind. Twisting and pulling out the Northern Horse Mussels, *Modiolus modiolus* L., takes patience and strong fingers, for they attach themselves deeply and strongly by their wiry byssus. In among the seaweed you are sure to find plenty of the pretty, tiny Northern Yellow Periwinkles, *Littorina obtusata* L.

Most prized of all will probably be the beautiful Atlantic Plate Limpet, *Acmaea testudinalis* Müller. You will have to look sharply at the pool edges and deeper in on the bottom, to see the 1-inch to $1\frac{1}{2}$-inch-long oval creatures, gray-brown with irregular streaks or bars, so perfectly matching the brownish bottom that they are almost impossible to see even as you stare at them. The interior is a lovely bluish-white, darker at center. Insert your knife quickly, before they detect danger, or you may break the shell in loosening it from its suction-hold on the rock. In twenty minutes of looking you should be able to find at least half a dozen.

Part of the charm of this trip is in the locality itself, for at Halibut Point Reservation you really get away from things. It is simple to take a lunch of tuna fish sandwiches and coffee, so that you need not hurry away, but can relax in some chosen nook of rock, or just lie flat and gaze at the ocean. On a warm summer day there may be swimmers in case you care to join them.

59. MYSTIC SEAPORT

It has been traditional in churches all over the world to use a large seashell as a baptismal font. The shell most frequently used in this way is probably the Giant Clam, often imported from the Philippines at some cost because of its thickness and weight. But the entirely unique baptismal font in plate 59, made of a single univalve, is to be seen, among other entertaining sights, at the town of Mystic Seaport, Connecticut.

The name Mystic Seaport might suggest something in the nature of a pirate treasure. Its origin is less romantic, since it gets its name from nearby Mystic, a celebrated old New England seafaring town strategically situated, for visitors, halfway between Boston and New York. In the warmer months, Mystic Seaport is a Mecca for visitors who like to get close to the things of the sea in a fascinating day's outing.

Actually this life-size exhibition of an old fishing, shipbuilding, and whaling town has been reconstructed on a piece of land near the mouth of the Mystic River. It is on the exact site where a George Clark and a Thomas Greenman had a prosperous shipyard in the early 19th century. Near the end of the first quarter of our century, however, life had taken a turn away from the old activities and

59. Shell Font at Mystic Seaport.
Photograph by Louis S. Martel, Courtesy of Mystic Seaport.

customs. The whole way of living in such a port was fading into the past. It was then that the idea of preserving the outward appearance of this bit of fascinating history was put into effect. Some local buildings were preserved. Others were moved in. Friends and strangers contributed nautical gifts from all over the eastern seaboard. Such gifts continue to come in, assured of protection and exhibition. There are ship models, figureheads, scrimshaw, harpoons, pistols, sextants, lanterns, compasses, and a fascinating collection of things once important as a part of life for the people of the sea. Along the wharfside are several famous vessels, to be observed or visited. Most famous of these is the *Charles W. Morgan,* a three-masted whaling ship which for eighty years sailed world seas. The last survivor of the great whaling ships, the *Charles W. Morgan* had made thirty-seven long whaling expeditions when it was towed in from its last voyage. It is a square-rigger, built of live oak and copper fastened. On its very first voyage to the Pacific it took fifty-three sperm whales. These were converted, right on board, into valuable whale oil, and stored in barrels such as those to be seen on the wharfside beside the ship.

Visitors may walk right on board this fabulous ship, inspect its whaling equipment, its dining cabin, and its galley. It is impressive, while on board, to realize that this very ship sailed, for many years, out of San Francisco to Japan and the Okhotsk Seas, and is estimated to have earned $2 million.

Of the many buildings worth a visit just a few are listed here. First there is the general store, with traditional cracker-barrel and apple basket. There is also a one-room school, with children's desks and an iron stove. Fishtown Chapel is a serene little white building, with a New England steeple. For seventy years it stood on the New London road, a few miles outside of Mystic. In the chapel is to be seen the unusual baptismal font.

The shell of which the font is made is a huge member of the Volutidae family. This is one of the Melon shells, so-called because of its resemblance to a melon. It is sometimes called *Melo aethiopica,* but more properly *Cymbium aethiopica.* (Since it comes, probably, from the Philippines, it is hard to say why it has a name that means "Ethiopian.") It is mounted on a carved wooden pedestal on which is found this inscription: "In memory of Captain Daniel Averill, Brandford, Conn. From his grandson Harold Daniel Hodgkinson." Shell fanciers should remember to drop into the chapel to see this font. It is but one of the many things that make a fine summer's day spent at Mystic Seaport one of the most rewarding visits a family can make in beautiful New England.

60. A SEASHELL AT
THE LIBRARY OF CONGRESS

One of the last places a person might expect to see an interesting seashell is at the Library of Congress in Washington, D.C. Yet in front of the Library of Congress Building is a replica of a magnificent shell, larger than life, part of a bronze sculptural group in which the seashell is being blown as a trumpet by the demigod Triton.

The larger figure in the bronze group is Neptune, who is seated in an appropriate regal posture. Son of the Titans Chronos and Rhea, he is, from the point of view of our culture, a very old god, called Poseidon by the Greeks. He reigned as god of the sea, and of the watery element in general.

The Romans called him Neptune, and also attributed to him the task of ruling over the waves of the sea and calling up or calming the tempests that plague all mariners. His fish-spear is his royal scepter, symbol of his total command of all matters concerning the sea, which presumably included fish and mollusks. His worship was early introduced into Rome, and on July 23 of every year he was honored by feasts and celebrations known as the Neptunalia.

In some peculiar way his name got flung into space, as if he were an early astronaut, and attached to one of the

60. Triton Blowing His Trumpet (Statuary Group, Library of Congress Building, Washington, D.C.).

planets. Just how this happened would be hard to say. Possibly the scientists had used up so many names like Mercury, Mars, Venus, and Saturn that they were hard put to find names for new-found planets.

Triton, shown blowing the shell trumpet, was the son of Poseidon, and was popularly supposed to be something of a merman, the lower half of his body being like that of a fish. Later, debased forms of Greek mythology imagined many Tritons, but properly there was just one. The fact that he was the blower of the shell trumpet by which Neptune's directions were telegraphed abroad over the ocean resulted in his name being transferred to that genus of shells known as the Tritons. It is particularly applied to one of the best known of all seashells, the Triton Shell, *Triton tritonis* L. (now called *Charonia tritonis* L.). This shell is traditionally regarded as the one that the demigod Triton used as a trumpet.

Now comes the switch. The shell that is cast in the sculptural set at the Library of Congress is not the customary Triton Shell of classical antiquity. On the contrary, it is that very American shell, the Pink Roller or *Strombus gigas* L., and its home is the waters off Florida and the West Indies. Its use in the statuary group might be called the Americanization or perhaps the internationalization of Neptune and Triton.

Whatever the actual intention of the sculptor was, he managed to bring Neptune up to date, and to show him as a god, not only of Greek and Roman seas, but also of the waters that wash our Atlantic coasts. Thus what might first appear as an incongruity may perhaps be just a modernization.

All people, from all times, have attempted some explanation of the forces and forms of nature which affect our lives and awaken our curiosity and wonder. The Greek and Roman stories of the gods and heroes were attempts to explain natural history, natural forces, and human emotions and behavior, and to help in controlling them.

Doubtless these ancient peoples were as proud of, and as vain about, their world picture as we are about ours. We should remember that a thousand years from now we shall appear to our descendants just as naive in our world picture of atomic fission and space travel as the Greeks and Romans appear to us. All world pictures are only the passing dreams of the times. It takes a sculptor, portraying a *Strombus gigas* instead of a *Triton tritonis,* to remind us that our own knowledge is not eternal.

61. SCANNING PADRE ISLAND

When you see a sign reading *Padre Island* you will be visiting part of the Texas coast until recently out of reach of most Americans. Now it is the nearest bit of seacoast for shell hunters who live in the Southeast, or in such distant states as Minnesota and North Dakota. Little known to most residents of the United States, this long, narrow island stretches parallel to the mainland shoreline along almost half of the long southern coast of Texas. On the shore side it forms the bay called Laguna Madre. On the other side, toward the Gulf of Mexico, is its seemingly interminable sandy beach.

To take in its extent one should glance at a map which will show that it is continuous from a point on the coast near Victoria all the way down to Brownsville on the Mexican border. But most of the southern part of this narrow strip is relatively inaccessible, so that on AAA maps the road is described in a box as "not advisable, dependent on low tide."

There is little doubt that, in coming years, Padre Island will be increasingly visited by holiday adventurers. This is ensured by the fact that it has become one of the National Seashores of the United States. Each of these seashores is very distant and different from the others.

61. Heading for Padre Island.

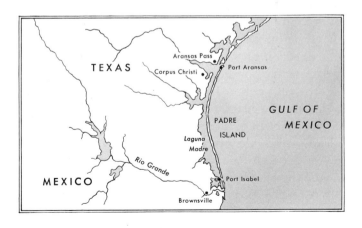

Point Reyes, in California, and Cape Cod, in Massachusetts, lie near to large cities. Padre Island is relatively remote.

Padre Island is the longest undeveloped segment of seashore in the United States, 117 miles in length. It is about 3 miles wide at its widest point, but only an eighth of a mile where it is narrowest; a short, if pointless, walk from coast to coast. The island is subtropical, being hot in summer and mild in winter. It is close to a part of the country now growing rapidly as a winter resort.

The waters of the Gulf of Mexico abound in fish and waterfowl. The land consists of grass-covered dunes between the two shorelines, the chief vegetation being sea-oats, croton, and morning glory. Native birds include the Red-winged Blackbird, the Wilson Plover, Egrets, the Little Blue and the Great Heron, Pelicans, the Laughing Gull, and the Black Skimmer.

Other visitors need considerably more guidance than I had when I visited Padre Island late in August. Careful inspection of a map will make it clear that the would-be visitor must choose with care his point of approach, since the island can only be reached by bridge or ferry. Without direction one may drive for hours to no purpose whatever. It is possible to cross to the island far south, near Brownsville, at Port Isabel, or to cross way up the coast near Corpus Christi, or where I entered by ferry at Port Aransas. The most accessible part of the coast of the long island parallels the paved road connecting the two entry points between Aransas Pass and Corpus Christi. The road just mentioned is deceptive, however, for it must be left by a side road if you are to get to the actual shore.

Turning off at one of these side exits, I was able to take a swim and collect a few coquinas before my time ran out.

There are a number of shell enthusiasts in some of the towns near the island, and they are very knowledgeable about the local seashells. It may also be helpful to visit the Corpus Christi Chamber of Commerce, for some advice on shelling. A collection of local shells exhibited at the Junior Museum in the same city gives the collector some notion of what he might be able to find. Most of the local species may be collected at relatively accessible points. The well-known favorite *Fasciolaria gigantea* Kiener, the Horse Conch, is sometimes taken in the vicinity of the lighthouse on South Padre. Many shrimp boats may be seen moored at Port Aransas, and they have at times brought in some deepwater shells.

62. ATLANTIC TO PACIFIC

The geography of Mexico is a decisive factor for everyone who takes a trip to that country. Except for Californians, who like to travel down the West Coast, where seashells are plentiful, most Americans find that their destination should be the high tablelands and mountains in and near Mexico City. This mountainous central area puts Mexico far ahead of all other places as a vacationland for Americans. It is unmatched for accessibility.

Any day of the year, winter as well as summer, and from any place in North America, it is possible (and I should say advisable) to take off in the family car on magnificent express highways right to the heart of Mexico. Within Mexico itself is a superb network of paved roads. Nowhere in the world is there such a panorama of incredibly scenic spots to be reached on paved roads, instead of by trek and tramp.

Because Mexico is so relatively narrow, it is possible to reach both the Atlantic and Pacific coasts within a few days. For me, the secret of mobility in Mexico is to choose Cuernavaca, near Mexico City, as a place of residence, using hotel, motel, or a rented apartment or house. One summer I stayed there with a friend who has a home near the ancient Aztec pyramid Teopanzolco. Every morning

62. Shell booth on the Malecon, Acapulco.

I experienced a never-failing lift to my spirits on stepping out to the sun to breathe the fresh mountain air and look up to the snowy peaks of towering Popocatepetl.

For vacationers this is one of the prime spots on the face of the globe, because, though people seem unwilling to believe it, Cuernavaca has a fine day every day of the year, with temperature always about seventy degrees. It is ideal for a visit just any time it is possible to get away.

So, although one of my main goals in visiting Mexico is to collect seashells, I prefer to live inland in Cuernavaca. From there, any day I care to I can take off down the mountains and, in five hours, experience that moment of exhilaration which comes inevitably as the coastal hills near Acapulco suddenly part to a view of the gleaming blue sea.

On arrival I take to air-conditioning in a small Swiss inn near the beaches. Each afternoon the fishermen bring in their nets on a nearby beach. Divers scour the sea bottom for shellfish which provide local markets and restaurants with food for gourmets.

It takes time and persuasion to prevail on the divers to bring up any specimen shells. But short-time visitors can have quite a holiday by visiting the shops and stalls along the Malecon, that fascinating waterfront parade, with its fabulous mixture of human and marine life. If you know a good shell when you see one you are sure to find a few surprising species and gather in a small collection of Pacific specimens.

The Atlantic coast is just as easy to reach from Cuernavaca. One year I stopped over at Fortin de las Flores, famed for its orchids and gardenias, and there were plenty of them. I lived a while at the amazing Posada Loma, set in one of the finest tropical gardens in the world. Here another superb volcano, Orizaba, is in sunlit view during breakfast. From Fortin it is only two hours down the steep mountainsides to hot Veracruz. The beaches there yield up some shells after a storm, but a scouring of the stalls near the wharves gives quicker results. There they specialize in shellcraft, and it is painful to see the best specimens of Tritons and Cowries cut up and fastened to plaster bases. I was still able to get some fine specimens of such shells as *Strombus raininus* and *Cassis testiculus,* which, added to my hoard from Acapulco, made a nice Atlantic-Pacific collection.

63. THE SEASHELLS
OF ACAPULCO

Of the thousands of visitors to Mexico's top resort, Acapulco, many are shell collectors. Many more might begin collections if they knew how. The trick is to use not only the beaches near the heart of the town, Caleta and Los Hornos, but to go a little farther along the shore to Puerto Marques. Here it is easy to combine swimming, sunbathing, and shell collecting.

When I first visited Puerto Marques, years ago, there was not a shell in sight. The beach on that magnificent bay was just as it is today. It is, without doubt, one of the best bathing beaches in the whole world, and I have tried many of them, the Lido in Venice, Suez, Colombo in Ceylon, and many another. Since the bay is almost a lagoon of blue salt-water it never has huge, dangerous breakers, just fine, rolling swells, ideal for swimming. The sand is smooth, the beach never overcrowded. The water is of that ideal temperature which cools but never chills, and it is good for as many hours as you care to linger.

Today, exactly as it was over a decade ago, the beach is bordered by a line of primitive, palm-thatched huts (*ramadas*) supported by poles. Here live Mexican families, each with a few rough tables and a kitchen to serve

63. She sells seashells at Puerto Marques; fresh-caught *Tonna ringens* Swain.

tortillas, fried fish, and soft drinks. You are free to use the hammocks and beach chairs, as it is assumed that you will buy something or other before you leave.

Perhaps you will buy some shells. For, surprisingly enough, all along the curb fronting the huts you will find little stands or stalls piled with shells in mild disarray. Often I have made raids on these stands. A good deal of bargaining went on, for bargaining is part of the fun of making friends with these agreeable people.

Shells in stock vary from stand to stand, and from season to season. Usually you have little trouble in finding superb specimens of the Grinning Tun Shell, *Tonna ringens* Swainson, of *Strombus galeatus* Sowerby, and of *Strombus gracilior* Sowerby, the plain *Strombus*. There is a prime chance to get unusually colorful specimens of the iridescent Blue Abalone, *Haliotis fulgens* Philippi. Good specimens of this shell must be hand picked from many to get shells of fine form and color. I have bought a dozen or more at a time in the old Acapulco market, from stands at Pie de la Cuesta nearby, and even from a lad who unstrung them from a cord on the sidewalk on a lane back from the waterfront. No one can make a mistake by buying half a dozen or so, for they are always welcomed as gifts to friends. Acapulco is an easy place to pick up shells, either to improve or even to start a collection.*

* Much has changed since the above was written. Now shells are scarce in and about Acapulco.

64. THE SHELL BOATS
OF ACAPULCO

Having come back to Cuernavaca from a visit to Acapulco, I write this account of the Shell Boats of Acapulco while the vision is still fresh in my memory. Acapulco is undoubtedly the prime winter resort of the Americas. Just as Europeans have flocked for generations to winter on the Riviera, so Americans are learning that their true winter goal is Mexico, including Guaymas, Mazatlan, Veracruz and, queen of them all—Acapulco.

The Christmas holidays bring on a vast rush to Acapulco. Mexicans themselves, finding Mexico City a little cold in December, flock to the beaches at sea level. Many from the United States with a Christmas vacation make a quick dash in by plane, and fill the hotels with a gay crowd. The shell hunters among them are usually unprepared for the opportunity of adding to their collections with little effort and small cost, and as a mere sideline to a magnificent winter holiday. Collectors sometimes have a vague hope that they can personally gather shells at Acapulco. This is virtually an impossible dream for visitors who stay only a few days.

Acapulco is a hilly peninsula surrounded by stunningly blue bays, roving beaches, and vast expanses of the Pacific. The waters at the beaches are alive with bathers and with

64. Shell Boat, Caletilla Beach, Acapulco.

small sailboats. Back roads, as far as Pie de la Cuesta on one side of the city and Puerto Marques on the other, look down over precipitous cliffs which make the shore-line almost inaccessible.

The only shells I have picked up in Acapulco I found at Revolcadero Beach, where the towering waves and vigorous undercurrents forbid swimming and diving. The simplest way to get a few shells in a short time is to head for the morning beaches, Caleta and Caletilla, which will probably be your earliest destination anyway. The sun shines brightly, but not too brightly, at nine in the morning, when all things are well under way at these two beaches. Caleta and Caletilla are adjacent, actually continuous beaches, just at the end of Acapulco's main boulevard along the waterfront. They are thus extremely accessible by car, by bus, and on foot.

The water is virtually always calm and quiet, and every day of the year, in the cooler parts of the day, morning and evening, these beaches are full of life. You settle down at the upper edge of the beach in a beach chair, where you can leave your towel and impedimenta. When the chair man arrives you pay him two pesos (about sixteen cents) as he attaches your ticket to the top of your chair. Your first desire will be to swim. As you paddle around, a narrow boat with a flat top may pass by, directed by a man tanned by sun and ocean. The top of his boat will be covered with things gathered from the sea. As you look you will note branches of white coral, perhaps a few sea urchins, and maybe some shells.

Gazing about, you notice, pulled up on the sand, one or two similar boats, beached and covered with shells.

Later on you will discover still others at the far end of the adjacent beach. Take a little time to explore, and you will find that the shell boats have quite a selection of local shells, caught by divers and spread out for display and sale. The boat in plate 64 shows, at one end, branches of coral, next a display of the local pearl shells, several of the Black *Murex,* and quite a few black-skinned *Anadaras.*

On each boat, and each day, the display will be a little different. Unusual discoveries are few and far between. But if you are lucky you might pick up a good-sized specimen of the Tent Olive, *Olivia porphyria.*

You now have to face some frustration. Most of the bivalves will have only one valve of the two, each valve unmatchable. It will take quite a while in the blazing sun, but gradually you may assemble a little mound of *Haliotis fulgens, Murex nigritus, Cardium consors,* and some bivalves you won't know the names of.

Now comes the bargaining. Ask how much each shell is, and you will be given a price. Pick out the shells you want, inspect every shell for breaks or unmatched pairs, put them in a pile, and make an offer. This may be less than half of the total asked, but if something more is demanded just accept and pay up. You may have to pay a little more proportionally for some shells, a little less for others, as the vendor has his own notion of shell values.

In any case, do the best you can. And you would have to be a very poor bargainer indeed to leave without quite a little inexpensive haul. You may even get a magnificent Grinning Tun (*Tonna ringens*) and a lovely yellow, globular *Cardium elatum.* Each year I find something different. And though the sun is hot, the chase is exhilarating.

65. BLUE CRABS ARE TO EAT

It may seem odd that the Blue Crab could be both a way of life for a man, and the chief support of his family, but so it is with Jesus Torre. I discovered this recently on an off-beat trip to Tuxpan, in eastern Mexico. It was a trip on which I planned to hunt for seashells, but I found myself at the edge of a soft-blue, South-Sea-Island type of lagoon, catching blue crabs with a dip-net borrowed from Jaime, the ten-year-old son of Mr. Torre.

This lagoon at La Barra is quite a little distance from the city of Tuxpan. At first I hesitated to take my car onto the beach, which runs as far as the eye can see in either direction. But my fear was groundless. All I had to do was follow the tracks of other cars and trucks for ten miles on the hard-packed sand of the upper beach, a veritable highway stretching along the line of lightening clouds and rolling sea. In the softness of the early morning light it was a drive to remember.

The beach ends at La Barra. There one may take a launch along the lagoon to Tamiahua, or whistle for a boat to cross the lagoon to the sand bar. I whistled, and soon Jaime was poling me across in a light boat which he pulled up into what was actually the bosom of his family.

Back off the beach was a bit of thatching on a few poles

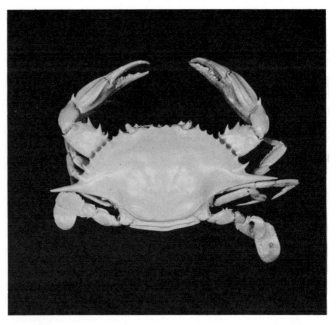

65. Blue Crab.

into which Mrs. Torre and the six children retreated occasionally. Outside was a bit of cloth giving shade over a table at which to eat. Nearer the shore, where we had landed, at the edge of the sand was a *ramada,* a palm-thatched shelter set up on slim poles.

Although the sun was tropical, shade came from above, and a cool breeze from the sides. There were two hammocks to swing in, packing cases to sit on, and the sand itself to lie on. The babies playing about at the water's edge were naked, the rest of us naked to the waist, for here was never a fly, never a single mosquito. I asked Mr. Torre why. His answer was, "Plenty of air." This nobody would deny.

Here was real escape. No spot could seem more remote, more exotic. Sitting, we watched the fishermen at the water's edge mending their nets, the babies splashing and laughing in the water. In the distance, below the thatched edging of the *ramada,* was the quiet lagoon, with a far line of jungle beyond it, and the misty mountain peaks forming a background like that in a Gauguin painting.

But one cannot dream forever, and the sea beaches on the far side of the sandbar were a challenge to action. An hour's wandering discovered much to amuse a beach-comber—an occasional starfish, antler-like roots of sea kelp, silver-tipped, horny scales of the Tarpon, plenty of those orbed sea shells *Dosinia discus* Reeve and *Dosinia elegans* Conrad. Back again at the lagoon, swimming was in and out. One hardly noticed which, since water seemed as much one's element as air. As one waded, the blue crabs scuttled about in all the beauty of their magnificently colored blue claws.

The crabs played a main part in this life of Señor Torre and his family, I learned in the easygoing friendliness of the *ramada,* the Torres' palm-thatched hut. The two Torre sons darted back and forth along the rim of the lagoon with nets on poles. Scoop, scoop, and it was another blue crab, or maybe two. Into the wicker basket they popped, and were counted—ninety-two, ninety-three, ninety-four—until the full quota was reached. This amounted to thirty dozen each morning, and thirty dozen more each evening. The trucks across the lagoon picked them up twice a day for the tables and restaurants of big Mexican cities far away. Since trucks paid a peso a dozen, here were riches and a pleasant life at the edge of the lagoon.

Hospitably, Mr. Torre invited me to lunch, and we were soon seated at the table. It was set out with ice cold Coca-Cola (cooled on ice brought in the trucks for the catch), fresh made tortillas, roast crabs, and crabs stewed, I regret to say, with more than a touch of garlic. It was the middle of a perfect day, a veritable saga of the Blue Crab.

66. SEASHELLS IN
AN INCREDIBLE
MEXICAN MUSEUM

It is surprising to discover the extent to which seashells can interpenetrate and become part of a culture. To realize this one has only to study the exhibits in the incredibly beautiful Museum of Anthropology in Mexico City's Chapultepec Park. The grandeur of this museum is unsurpassed. Its twenty-three exhibit halls are arranged around a vast, oblong inner patio. At the near end of this patio is a gigantic umbrella or wheel-top fountain, which stands on one central pillar. The high ring of this fountain sheds, from its edge, a heavy rainfall upon the basinless floor of tile.

A giant model of a seashell, in concrete, forms the second accent and is found at the far end of the same patio. Thus are symbolized the rainy sky, the fertile land, and the teeming sea of the Mexican paradise. Thus introduced, the seashell motif runs, like a minor theme, through most of the many folk cultures forming the subject-matter of the exhibits.

One must be alert and watch carefully if one is to isolate and observe the seashells, because they are mixed in with exhibits so fascinating as to divert and hold one's attention. Prominently displayed and large enough not to be missed in the very first introductory salon, is a

66. Museum of Anthropology, Mexico City.

giant Ammonite fossil, of primeval antiquity. It is actually three feet across. In the same room, less challenging to the eye, yet worth looking at, may be seen an ancient *Arca*. In another case is a fantastic and very old necklace decorated with several "Egg" shells, *Amphiperas ovum* L. Their presence poses an interesting problem, since this shell is not from Mexican waters but is of Indo-Pacific origin. In still another case is a moneybag decorated with money cowries, presumably from a time and place in which these shells were used as money.

Passing from room to room one is astonished and dazzled at the outpouring of art and artistic capacity. These are seen in the huge color murals and paintings, in the ethnic models of various races of Indians in their home settings, and in figures of tribal dances with a live musical background of recorded music. Myriads of artifacts are perfectly displayed in glass cabinets, some of which hang from swinging supports attached to the ceiling.

It would be tedious to trace through the location of each display of seashells. Somewhere along the way, however, may be seen all of the following. Of several necklaces, one is of cone-shaped cuttings, probably from a small strombus. Others from the remote Seri tribe of West Mexico are made up of *Cerithium* shells and several cones, among them *Conus ximines* and *Conus mahogani*. Still another necklace, from the area of Chihuahua and Sonora, is composed of small *Cerithium* shells.

Shell jewelry of many kinds is to be seen in various exhibits. On display are bracelets, pectorals, pendants, and rings. From the Seris is another unusual necklace composed of olive shells and *Anomia* shells. This was probably once used in religious ceremonies to exorcise sickness.

A horn fabricated from a shell beautifully ornamented with turquoise and a wide bracelet both orginated on the West Coast. From inland Guanajuato came a small scallop formed into a pendant; and from San Miguel Allende are several birds cut out of shells as ornaments. Occasionally a human form is seen, also cut out of a bit of shell. A special cabinet in the Hall of the Huastecas is devoted to shell artifacts. This cabinet contains a series of rings, faces, ornaments, and a remarkable cameo cut in reverse.

Oddments are found here and there throughout the museum. Some of the most striking are ancient specimens of the Tented Olive, *Oliva porphyria* L., carved specimens of a huge *Fasciolaria,* and an amazing ornament, set with a mosaic of colorful abalone shell and made into the form of a lynx head, in the open mouth of which is a man's face. Shells used as plates to hold powdered, colored cosmetics are to be seen in one of the cases.

The museum itself, one of the most rewarding in the world, is on the far side of upper Paseo de la Reforma, Mexico City's grand boulevard. This avenue splits Chapultepec Park into two sections. It may be reached by bus or taxi, or an automobile may be parked in the huge parking lots. Many American visitors, used to all-day museums, fail to note the open hours, and so spoil their visit. The museum is closed on Monday, and open Tuesday through Friday, from 10 A.M. to 2 P.M., at which time it is closed tight, but reopens at 4 P.M. and stays open to a late 8 P.M. The admission is nominal. On Saturdays, Sundays, and holidays the museum is open from 10 A.M.

to 6 P.M. Cameras may be used on payment of a substantial fee. The restaurant is a somewhat shaky Automat. (The day my wife and I ate there, there were no liquids of any kind.) But it is open from 10 A.M. to 9 P.M., even on Mondays, and is a refuge when the exhibits are closed. Thus it is a good place to dally and wait among the beautiful green surroundings of ancient Chapultepec Park. Never hot, never cold, this is one museum that can be enjoyed in perfect comfort.

67. SHELL HOUSE
AT TECOLUTLA

Seashell collectors are where you find them, and that may be almost anywhere and in all countries of the world. J. K. Grosch has his fine collection in Mozambique, East Africa. Julian Dashwood has a world collection in his South Pacific Polynesian paradise in the Cook Islands. The colorful collection of Don Carlos Prieto, which I have visited and studied, is in the microscopically tiny town of Tecolutla, on the Atlantic coast of Mexico.

Tecolutla is at the mouth of a river which runs out to flat sand coast stretching thirty miles in both directions north and south. Don Carlos has his own magnificent home in Mexico City, almost up against the famed two-color home of Mexico's most famous artist, the late Diego Rivera. But, like many of us in the United States, Don Carlos also has a country home, and for this he chose the fertile coastland stretching north from Veracruz to Tampico. It is a wild land, ideal for hunting and for all kinds of boating and deep-sea fishing. The coastal people are, for the most part, fisher folk, and theirs is a sea tradition. From his home base in Tecolutla Don Carlos has been able to develop vast acreages of coconut palms, lining the coastal strip in great magnificence for many miles. Inland are his orange groves, their countless trees laden with enough fruit for much of Mexico.

67. Shell House at Tecolutla, Veracruz.

If you roam these tropical beaches in summer, as I have done repeatedly, you will find few shells, only an occasional bivalve or a few sand collars. But in January and February, when wild storms blow along the coast, shells are torn from the deep and are cast up on the endless miles of sandy shore. After such storms, who can resist a little beachcombing? Thus Don Carlos began what has grown into his present superb collection.

This collection has made, of the Tecolutla house shown in plate 67, almost a small shell museum. Set out in the living room, in especially designed glass cabinets, is a magnificent collection of both local and world shells. Some of the prizes of the collection are a complete exhibit of shells of the local coast, all labeled and set forth in series in wall cases. I am grateful to Don Carlos for his gift of a complete set of photographs of this collection, which includes all the shells of the locality. Among them are the elusive deep sea Lamp Shell, *Xancus angulata* Solander, and a huge Horse Conch, *Fasciolaria gigantea* Kien. One of the most startling shells is a *Cassis tuberosa* L., a King Helmet so large that it is almost too heavy to lift.

The central cabinet, set as a low glass-topped table in the center of the living room, is bright with color specimens from everywhere, like the gold and purple *Pecten nobilis,* as well as *Conus virgo, Oliva porphyria,* a huge Paper Nautilus, and some flashy Australian Volutes. Here is one of the few collections used as a superb form of basic interior decoration, a remarkable feature of this unique seacoast home.

68. A SHELL COLLECTION
FOR MEXICO

Time Magazine for July 27, 1962 carried a note reporting
the purchase of the German Borgward automobile assets
by "Millionaire Mexico City Lawyer Ernesto Santos
Galindo." It was my privilege to be entertained one
summer at the beautiful home of Licenciado Galindo on
Lake Tequesquitengo, a two-hour drive south of Mexico
City.

There Don Ernesto was developing what has probably
become the most extensive collection of shells to be found
in Mexico. His interest in shells began suddenly the
previous winter, during an automobile trip to Key West,
Florida. There he bought a number of shells, starting off
his collection with a *Turritella terebra*. From Florida he
and his party took a tour of the Caribbean and, as the
tour progressed, other shells were obtained in Jamaica,
Haiti, and Saint Thomas in the Virgin Islands. From this
small beginning grew what must have been one of the
most rapidly assembled collections of all time.

Each weekend during my visit, when Don Ernesto
returned from Mexico City he brought with him a pile
of boxes that had arrived by mail, stuffed with shells. It
was prime entertainment to help him unpack each
treasure-trove to see what it contained—how varied it
was, how colorful, of what quality, size, and beauty.

The alcove in the pavilion began to fill up rapidly. To

68. Huge Queen Helmet Shell (*Cassis madagascarensis*) at
Tequesquitengo.

one side, on a specially built combination of shelves and drawers of polished wood, was set out a display of some of the more spectacular shells. Here were the all-time favorite, the Nautilus, with a split half beside it, showing chambers and canals; a fine pair of Angel Wings, *Cryptopleura costata* L.; a small *Thatcheria mirabilis* Angas; a *Murex triremis* Perry; a twisted *Latiaxis mawae* Griffith & Pidgeon; a *Voluta junonia* Shaw; a smooth aristocratic *Voluta aulica* Sowerby; and for a green accent, an Emerald Land Snail from Manus Island, in the Admiralty Islands.

On the very top shelf were the largest and finest specimens I had ever seen of *Cassis madagascarensis* L. They came from Champoton, Yucatan, a gift of Sr. Juan Lambreton, director of the shipyards at Vera Cruz. The largest is perfect, and thirteen inches long, enough to make quite an impression in any collection.

At right angles to the open display was a series of steel cabinets, with wide, smooth-running drawers. On top of the cabinets was an ever growing bookshelf of current and out-of-print books on shells. There was also a display of large shells, including two magnificent specimens of *Fasciolaria gigantea* Kiener, also from Sr. Lambreton; three Lamp Shells, *Xancus angulatus* Solander, from East Mexico; three of the East Coast Tritons, *Cymatium variegata* Lam. This group is flanked by beautifully pink specimens of *Strombus gigas* L. The display does honor to Vera Cruz and other East Coast Mexican states.

It was a pleasant surprise to pull out each of the cabinet drawers, where the shells are set out methodically in open transparent plastic boxes. The top drawer had an assortment of fifty and more spiny *Murex* shells, including the

West Coast Cabbage *Murex, Murex brassica* Lam.; *Murex nigritus* Philippi; and some of the fantastic *Muricidae* from other parts of the world, such as *Murex cornucervi* Röding. At that time there was room for growth in the *Murex* section and it was growing rapidly.

The second drawer had a startling collection of cowries, starring a few Map Cowries, *Cypraea mappa* L.; the Tortoise Cowry, *Cypraea testudinaria* L.; also some beautiful Mexican Stag Cowries or Micromacs, *Cypraea cervus* L. The cone drawer, with 300 cones, was filling up. It was dazzling with its accent of *Conus marmoreus* L., the Marble Cone, its beautiful Governor Cone, *Conus gubernator* Hwass, and its star of the show, a lovely *Conus genuanus* Hwass, from Senegal, West Africa. The Pectens, a drawer below, presented their usual brilliant array. They required some filling out, but were, like the whole collection, growing fast. All these shells, approximately two thousand species, had been assembled in a three-month period, through Don Ernesto's remarkable ability at organizing, arranging, and remembering.

Since that first time, I have visited Licenciado Galindo on recent return trips to Mexico. In the interim Don Ernesto has prepared a notable exhibit, in a series of glass display cases, of practically all the shells shown in Hugh and Marguerite Stix's 1963 book, *The Shell*. He has also added to his collection such rarities as *Strombus goliath* Schröter and the Golden Cowry. He showed me the architect's plans for a shell museum and I have since received a letter saying that it was being built, at the Tequesquitengo lakeside.*

* The Museum, now complete, has many notable accessions.

V

PRACTICAL
SUGGESTIONS

69. HOW TO COLLECT SHELLS

There is no single reason why people collect shells. I have been asked over and over again, "Just how do you begin to make a collection?" The answer is: "Begin in any way at all in which you can get a few shells together, for there is no such thing as a prescribed collection that one should acquire in the beginning. A collection starts with a single shell. Every collection is individual, and each represents a person, his opportunities, and his taste."

Most collectors get started when they are near the seashore. Some beaches in Florida appear to be nothing but pulverized seashells, and dead shells may often be picked up on shores all over the world. But dead shells have lost their gloss and color, and are often chipped or abraded. Live shore mollusks are mostly found at dead low tide by wading in the water, or by discovering them near tide mark before the sea birds get first pick.

The best time for such searching is after a storm, just when most people tend to keep away from a windy beach. Almost any shell from the deeps may be cast up, at times, and taken while still alive. A specimen of the Juno's Volute, *Voluta junonia* Shaw, with the rare left-hand opening, picked up a winter or so ago on a Florida beach, made the newspapers as a feature story.

69. Any shells make a collection.

No one has the advantage of anyone else in this game, and an amateur might really have the edge if there is any such thing as "beginner's luck." The thrill of finding an unusual specimen has started many a person on the road toward a fine collection. One of the foremost collectors in Mexico, Don Carlos Prieto, started because he had a holiday home at Tecolutla, near Vera Cruz. From that base he organized a superb collection of the shells of that coast, and expanded it to a world collection. My wife's father, Alden Strong, began by specializing in the Crown Conch, *Melongena corona* Gmel., mostly from the shores of Lake Maggiore, in Florida. He gradually expanded his hoard until he developed a fine collection.

So one way to begin is just to bring home your tide-mark trophies, boil them, clean them, get the names from standard books or by matching up with specimens of friends who know shells, label and list each specimen on a filing card, and display your collection. Gradually the group takes form, but for you it is unique, because every shell becomes a memory of a time well spent at some intriguing beach or rocky promontory.

But alas, not everyone lives near the beach. There are, nevertheless, advanced shell collectors in Wisconsin, New Mexico, and Arizona, states which, magnificent as they are, are not known for their ocean playgrounds. Some of these inland collectors have shells sent them by relatives from coastal parts. Others buy their shells. One of the well-known collectors of the United States started by buying a harp shell from a case in the American Museum of Natural History in New York. Sooner or later, as they become self-educated, most serious collectors begin to buy shells from all over the world, for most mollusks favor a particular country.

Some of the most spectacular shells, like *Latiaxis mawae* Griffith & Pidgeon, come from a far country, in this case Japan. The handsome *Voluta hunteri* Iredale, once called *Voluta marmorata* Swainson, usually comes from Australia. The Cameo Shell, *Cassis rufa* L., and the Saffron Spider, *Lambis crocata* Link, usually come from East Africa. These shells are so different from others, except their relatives, that collectors usually yearn for them. In the end, therefore, all collections that grow to any size include shells that are bought or exchanged. It is harder, and more expensive, to travel to all the shores of the world, than it is to buy or exchange shells. The people of distant countries covet our shells, just as we do theirs. A *Voluta junonia* (seen in plate 69, shell at upper right, with black squares) is about on a par for scarcity and beauty with a *Voluta rutila* Broderip from Australia, so that the two may be exchanged one for one. Contacts are often difficult to make, however. And, at a given time, specimens of certain coveted shells are temporarily unobtainable. *Perotrochus hirasei* Pilsbry, from Japan, is, as I write, not available, although at the moment I know several people who are clamoring to buy one at a price of about eighty dollars. When one or two become available, the price might drop. So it is with rare shells.

Obviously a vast number of beautiful shells from all over the world can be gathered and displayed for the enjoyment of one's friends. But there is absolutely no fixed rule for making a collection. Whatever means leads to this excellent end is a good way to collect shells.

70. NAMING SHELLS

What has bullfighting to do with seashells? Not much, to be sure. But the shell shown in plate 70 was once named after a bullfighter, and a lady bullfighter at that! The story of how this happened is also a particularly useful example of the way in which a shell gets its name, and sometimes loses it.

Most people feel a bit uncomfortable with the shells they have collected until they have names for them. A successful collecting trip to the beach is usually followed by a session of cleaning, inspecting, beautifying, and arranging one's "catch." After the summer there may come a certain restless search, often continuing into the late fall, when there is less of the outdoors and more time for one's shell collection.

Shells displayed at home, or in school, or at a shell show must be correctly named, because each one, no matter how humble or how rare, is a part of today's super-scientific world. "Naming is knowing."

Beginners are apt to look around for a common name like Angel Wing or Moon Shell. This connects with what one already knows; it is a natural attempt to keep within the safe world of present experience, and avoid the discomfort of growing pains. In fact, many a mollusk may

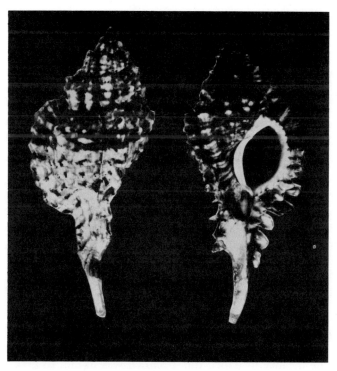

70. *Murex pulcher* A. Adams.

have a local common name that is good enough to start with but, in the end, will lead to confusion. The Cherrystone Clam, for instance, popularly served in one town on the half shell, in another may be called a Little Neck Clam and on Cape Cod a Quahog.

There are scores of scientists who study mollusks in every advanced country of the world—in Japan, in Australia, in Argentina—and most of them will never be able to visit an American beach. But all of them will have a name, just one name, the same name, for the clam in question, and that name is *Venus merceneria* L.

This name is in accordance with the binomial system of naming, now in universal use to name each plant and animal, no matter where in nature it occurs. The first name, *Venus,* is the "generic" name, the name of the group or genus to which this shell belongs. The second name, *merceneria,* is the "trivial" or species name of this mollusk, for no other *Venus* shell can have this name. *Linné* is the customary form of the name of Linnaeus, the great classifying biologist of the 18th century. Linnaeus first described this shell in writing and named it. He is therefore called the "author" or the "authority."

The scientific name of a mollusk is usually made up of the generic name, the trivial or species name, and the name of the authority. A label should give, in addition, the locality in which the specimen was found, to give a key to its natural living place and to help indicate the range in which it thrives. An old hand who seeks the name of a shell will get it from a friend who has a named specimen, or by looking up its picture and description in a standard book on shells.

But to get back to our bullfighter—the photograph shown here (plate 70) was sent to my wife's father by the late Hyatt Verrill, a second-generation conchologist, for his father was a shell expert and a professor at Yale University.

Hyatt Verrill had a granddaughter named Consuela, who was a bullfighter, and he was so proud of her that he named this particular mollusk after her, calling it *Murex consuela* Verrill. I have had several specimens of this rare and beautiful little shell from Soufrière, on Dominica Island, in the West Indies. But alas—how fickle is fame and a name! One day another scientist picked up a specimen of this shell and remembered that it had been named earlier by a Mr. Adams.

Now, the rule of scientific naming is that a name must be dropped if the same species has been described under a different name at an earlier date. Thus the correct name to date of this little shell is *Murex pulcher* A. Adams. Fortunately, something like this seldom happens, and the species name of most shells will never vary from the name found in shell books. For 95 per cent of species names have settled down, virtually for good.

One may comfort oneself that he may use any documented name he finds, and change the label when and if he likes. The shell remains the shell it was before the change. Some of us like certain names and won't change our labels in too much of a hurry. I am just unscientific enough and stubborn enough to file my card for the little shell in the picture under *Murex consuela,* adding a sad footnote, "now *Murex pulcher* A. Adams."

71. CONCHOLOGY OR
MALACOLOGY?

A shell collector will not be at his hobby long without coming across some other, grander name for his interest in shells. He has known that the study of birds is called ornithology, the study of insects is called entomology, and doubtless he has heard that the study of shells is called conchology. Unfortunately he cannot leave it at that, for he will not proceed very far in reading anything current about his hobby before he finds that the branch of biology which has to do with mollusks is called, not conchology, but malacology.

This has caused many a shell collector, if not sleepless nights, at least a rather long-lasting and nagging confusion. It is not even certain that, after reading the following explanation, some of this dismay will not remain.

The term *conchology* held complete sway for many years in earlier shell books. I have just been fortunate in being able to buy a very rare and wonderful book on mollusks, a classic on the subject. It is a two-volume work in French, published in 1863 in Paris. Step by step it goes through the whole kingdom of mollusks as it was then organized, giving the scientific names of over a thousand species including many of today's favorites, under names still in use, such as *Nautilus pompilius* L. for the Cham-

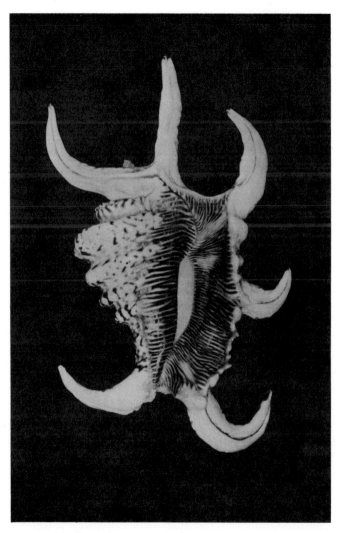

71. *Lambis chiragra arthritica* Röding.

bered Nautilus. The plates are superior steel engravings, some hand-colored, some showing the shell with its colorful animal living in it.

The book was written by a French scientist, Dr. J. C. Chenu, and the point to which I am leading is that it is called *Manual of Conchology*. Until about the end of the last century a scientific specialist in mollusks was called a conchologist. But now comes the villain of the piece. Sometime near the beginning of this century, someone, and his compeers, came up with another very respectable name, *malacology*.

Of the rival terms, *malacology* won, hands down. Today it has completely prevailed. It has even become something of a badge of merit, for being called a conchologist has come to convey the idea that one is a second-rate worker who has not the stamp of the mighty academic degree to go along with his other professional equipment.

Fortunately, present-day collectors do not have to choose between the two words, especially if they are content with the humble name of shell collector. The two scientific names come from Greek through Latin. *Conchology* is from the Latin *concha,* meaning "a seashell." *Malacology* is from the Latin *malacus,* meaning "soft or delicate." Thus we have the rejected term *conchology,* "a study of shells," and the approved term *malacology,* "a study of soft or delicate creatures."

There are those who, because they are sufficiently informed to merit being called naturalists in the area of mollusk shells, may, even today, quite properly be called conchologists. But the title "malacologist" places the man in the professional class, as does "biologist," or "atomic scientist." It may properly be reserved for those who enter the field of marine biology, a branch of science which is growing by leaps and bounds as we humans begin to notice that the sea is important for things other than floating ships.

On a recent trip to Washington I visited the Smithsonian Institution, one of the top scientific institutions of the country. My objective there was to seek the answer to a small matter involving the derivation of the name *Lambis,* which, as far as I have been able to conjecture, after consultation, seems to be "something that licks," like a flame. Not a satisfactory guess. The curators in the Department of Mollusks very kindly helped from their research resources in finding answers to all my questions. The Smithsonian collection is one of the world's finest, as well as one of the largest in the country. It is similar in type to others in our large universities such as that in the Department of Mollusks in the Harvard University Museum of Comparative Zoology and the Department of Mollusks of the American Academy of Natural Sciences in Philadelphia. These superb scientific centers are witness to the fact that malacology has been growing up. It has now become of age as a mature science, and a new field for many an ambitious student in coming years.

72. CLEANING SHELLS

Many a shell collector has begun his collection by picking up beach shells at the seashore. But if he goes a bit further with his studies he will discover that these are considered "dead" shells. At the edge of low tide, and just beyond the rocks, is a teeming population of living mollusks. These, as well as those from deeper water, are the interest of the true collector.

A beach shell may be worn and broken, bleached of its color and lacking in luster. Worse still, the two matching parts of bivalves may be separated, and one lost, making it impossible to get a complete specimen. Consequently careful collectors insist on specimens caught while alive. These are not only more interesting and valuable, but also more difficult to secure and to handle.

Every correctly labeled shell in a collection is not merely a shell. It is the result of a great deal of work and care, from the catching of the mollusk, to removing the animal inside the shell, cleaning the surface to improve the shell's appearance, identifying it by its scientific name, and labeling it with this name and the locality in which it was found.

If the specimen has come from a foreign land, it only gets to the collector after a considerable amount of cor-

72. Marble Cone before (left) and after cleaning.

respondence, and after being packed carefully and sent, usually by parcel post. Never despise a properly labeled, live-caught specimen of even a small or common shell, for it did not reach its showplace without a lot of labor and care.

Summer is a favorite collecting time for many. During the summer many a collector will find himself just back from the seashore with a catch of uncleaned shells, the odor still mild, but mounting. Something must be done, and quickly. This usually means that the shells must be boiled in a saucepan or tin can for about ten to twenty minutes. There is some danger of cracking or breaking, but it is not much with the less fragile shells. In lieu of boiling, shells may be frozen in the refrigerator for about seventy-two hours, during which time the animal shrinks and the muscles of attachment separate from the shell. On the shells' removal from the freezer, run cool tap water over them for five or ten minutes.

After either boiling or freezing, bivalves may be removed by scraping, univalves by placing a pronged instrument in the most fleshy part, and twisting; if parts break off they are hard to remove later, and become odorous in time. To free the remaining animal, fill the shell with water and stand it on its end overnight. Next day shake it out under running water. It may take quite a few days to clean stubborn shells thoroughly, but the water must be changed every day, since decaying animal matter makes an acid ruinous to the finish of the shell. Other ways of cleaning shells and greater detail on procedure will be found in the most complete discussion available, *How to Clean Sea Shells* (1966), a twenty-page booklet by Eugene Bergeron, Director of the Marine Biological Research Associates, Balboa, Canal Zone.

But now the cleaning process is hardly half over. Some few people like to keep their shells in the rough, as being more natural. But the average shell collector wants to show off his shells and likes to "put them through the beauty shop." The two specimens of the Marbled Cone, *Conus marmoreus* L., shown in plate 72 are brother and brother. They came to me in the same package with a dozen others from Zamboanga in the Philippines. The animals were removed before they were sent, probably by a system much used in the tropics—letting the ants do it. One specimen is shown in all its adhering mud and grime, the other in all its charm, revealed only after a rigorous cleaning.

The first step in such a cleaning is to soak the shell in laundry bleach of the type sold under the brand name of Clorox. After soaking the shell for several hours, or overnight, scrub off any loosened dirt and any periostracum, or "skin," under running water.

Lime deposits may be taken off by the use of water-diluted muriatic (hydrochloric) acid, which may sometimes be bought in a hardware store. This is a dangerous liquid and adults should be careful of it. Children should use it only under supervision. The acid must be kept in a glass or acid-resisting container. The shell should be immersed with tongs momentarily, and then plunged in a bucket of cold water and thoroughly rinsed. Lime spots that remain may be removed, in part, by a touch-up with dilute acid. Vaseline may first be used to cover any part of the shell that might be injured by the acid.

From there on a shell may be scraped and worked on until the best form and color are brought out. Many collectors even away the edge and straighten the lines with a file or a small electric drill. In fact, an avid collector will often work hours on a prized specimen until every form and color facet exhibits the very utmost in molluskan good looks.

73. PACKING SHELLS
FOR MAILING

Recently I received a huge box of popcorn from Ethiopia. Unfortunately, however, it was not edible. Stale from its five or six weeks' journey by sea, it had taken on the odor of some shells packed in it, half a dozen *Trochus dentatus* which the supplier had sent improperly cleaned. The popcorn was, of course, merely packing material, and very good packing material indeed. In it were safely nestled some shiny, spotted *Cypraea pantherina,* cowries which are scarce here because knowledgeable contacts in the Red Sea area are rare.

The packing of shells for shipment through the mails is a problem met by every person who goes farther than his own local beaches for shells. Shells are mailed by collectors, both to nearby and to distant places such as New Zealand, Papua, or the Marshall Islands, and in fact to any port in which there is someone interested in shells. Shell exchanges are mailed back, but in this type of mailing there is heartbreak. From experience I think I could safely say that a quarter of the shells mailed by inexperienced packers come in broken. Of the huge boxes received from all over the world, not more than half of those from distant parts, even those from experienced packers, come in undamaged. Plate 73 shows

73. Packages of shells crushed in the mails.

the condition in which just two packages were received. Presumably they were crushed in steamship holds under heavy cases or handled by powerful machines in post offices, or tumbled among heavy boxes with sharp corners.

How often have we mourned some shell like the huge *Tonna cepa* that arrived with a half-inch-square hole in the body whorl, or a majestic *Triton* arriving from the Fiji Islands with the lip broken off? Hundreds of fine shells have arrived chipped, cracked, or crushed to bits.

My purpose is not, however, to bemoan a myriad broken shells, but to make some suggestions for packing which should serve all those who send shells by mail, or by any public carrier. Here is a set of rules which may not prevent all breakage but which nevertheless will save a lot of misery if observed.

1. The boxes used for packing must be of heavy construction. The thin light-cardboard boxes so often mailed are useless. Some of them arrive quite empty, all the shells having dropped out on the way! All boxes used must be of heavy, often corrugated material, fresh and unbent to start with.

2. Boxes must be reinforced, either by cross-pieces, or by lining with heavy, corrugated material. In some cases large boxes should be reinforced along four corners by the insertion of wooden posts tightly protecting the interior edges with strong uprights. But whatever means are used, the sender should be certain that the boxes are reinforced, since the perils of the voyage are tougher than you think. Whenever it is permitted, insure parcels to the country of destination, since, no matter how careful the packing, the loss is sometimes complete.

3. Boxes should be placed inside other boxes. This is virtually essential. Fragile shells must be separately packed, each according to its special characteristics, in its own strong box, the smaller boxes being then packed snugly in the larger box, and the separations between them padded with newspaper.

Tin cans, often used inside large boxes, are usually poor packing material, for they are often dented by a sharp blow. If used, they should be protected by newspaper and by careful placement in the package. Amateur packers often break the fragile shells in the very act of inserting them. I have received *Tibia fusus* thus packed, the needle-like points broken off against the sides of the can.

4. Usually everything should be wrapped in news-paper, two or more layers when needed. Occasionally fragile shells are wrapped in tissue paper. Spondylus shells, with their over-all frondlike spines, are sometimes buried in sawdust. In all packing it is most important to give careful consideration to what you are doing and avoid packing fragile edges to face the heavy, hard surfaces of other shells. Heavy shells do not pack well with light ones, and may even have to be mailed separately.

5. Pack tightly enough so that the total contents will not be crushed into a small space inside the box, and so tossed back and forth when being moved, until some shells crack against others. Yes, heavy packing does increase postage. But it pays many times over, in the long run, because everyone is dismayed by broken shells. Embarrassing questions are then asked, such as "How?" and, worse still, "Who?"

74. SHELL BOOKS
CAN HELP YOU

"You cannot get very excited about any class of shells without the books that go with them." This dictum was written by the late Walter Freeman Webb, a naturalist who did more than any other American to popularize shell collecting during the first half of the 20th century. In addition to a life work of amassing a large collection, and of importing and selling shells from remote countries, Webb wrote a number of books for collectors. For many years these were about the only practical handbooks used by non-professional collectors. Pictures were in black and white.

Until after World War II, color processes were not in use. Dammed up during the war, color printing reached us in an inundation during the last two decades. The only early color pictures of shells were to be found in the hand-colored plates of books by the great 19th-century conchologists like Swainson and Reeve.

Webb's books were organized for practical use. The illustrations of thousands of shells were, for the most part, reasonably accurate drawings, each with a thumbnail description conveniently placed on the opposite page. Because they crosscut the world in a day when books on shells were scarce, they sold by the thousands, and were to be found in the hands of almost all collectors at that time.

His *Catalogue of Recent Mollusca* is at this writing out of print but perhaps to be reprinted. The *Handbook for Shell Collectors,* however, is still currently available (Lee Publications: Framingham, Mass., 16th rev. ed., 1971). The plates are a bit worn from many reprintings, and the nomenclature not always of recent date, but the book makes possible the identification of many small shells difficult to find in any other book.

Webb was something of an independent soul, a rugged American individualist who went his own way. Perhaps, for this reason, he has not received the recognition he deserves in shelldom. (There is, perhaps, a tendency among some of the lesser lights among the malacologists, though never among the great ones, to snub collectors who lack professional academic degrees. Collectors should never feel inferior in the presence of a professional, because the true scientist is always more impressed by his own ignorance than by his knowledge.)

As witness to Webb's independence I have, in my papers, a long list of corrections of one of his books which was sent to him by the English naturalist Hugh Comber Fulton (1861–1942). In all the years in which that book was published Webb did not make one correction, even of the most egregious errors. This might be regarded as a bit of stubbornness, but perhaps it was because it is difficult to alter the plates of a book, once they have been made.

We might think of shell books as falling into one of four groups, given here in historical sequence:

This includes the works of the great conchologists of a century or more ago, among them the colossal series of Lovell Augustus Reeve who, with G. B. Sowerby, wrote the stupendous twenty-volume classic *Conchologica Iconica*. (There is a copy in the Boston Public Library.) The meticulous and admirable volumes of Swainson and those of the French conchologist Chenu are also in this first group. In a practical sense, these books may be superfluous for collectors. For anyone who likes shell books, however, it is a joy to seek them out in one of our great libraries or museums, and such an excursion is worth taking for its own sake.

GROUP TWO

This group includes the popularizing writing of Webb and some others. These were a standby for the first third of this century. Among them might be found *The Shell Book* (Charles E. Branford Co.: Newton Centre, Mass., rev. ed. 1951), a tome full of miscellaneous information on shells, somewhat haphazardly arranged. It was written by Julia Rogers, a New England lady of some fame, known also for her book *Captain January*, a popular tale made into a popular moving picture and later adapted to television.

Very useful were the books of Maxwell Smith. His *World-Wide Sea Shell and Rock Shell Catalogue* (1953), out of print since his death, is still the only book in English that can give the amateur help in getting the families and classes of mollusks into any kind of scientific order. Although it leaves the collector without benefit of subsequent changes in taxonomy and nomenclature, it has not yet been superseded. The section on *Muricidae,* the rock shells, is bound into copies of this book. It is still the only book with photographic illustrations of *Muricidae* from all over the world appearing in a single volume. This is also true of his *Review of the Volutidae* (Tropical Photographic Laboratory: Lantana, Fla., 1942), recently updated and distributed by the Borden Publishing Company of Alhambra, California.* All these books were helpful because they show specimens found in many countries. They were the work of naturalists rather than professional biologists, but the photographs and drawings in black and white were a boon to those who could afford only a small library. They were the books of an era which, though it is long past, is not to be despised.

GROUP THREE

This group of books on shells is composed of new scientific works, splendid books written for the specialist, rather than for the general collector. They represent the attempt to get mollusks into scientific control by the careful study of groups of shells, or of some special family or marine locality.

Among the earlier of these are the books of the late Joyce Allan, an Australian. There is much enthusiasm for

* *The Living Volutes* by C. C. Weaver and John E. duPont (Museum of Natural History: Greenville, Dela., 1970) was published after these lines went to press.

shells, and there are some great collectors and collections in Australia. Unfortunately little is heard about them in other parts of the world. In the days when there was much chaos in malacology, Joyce Allan struggled patiently with almost insurmountable problems, to write what is, even now, the only book covering the world of cowries as it was known at the time. It is replete with plates, some in color, providing illustrations, not photographs, of most of the cowries then known.

Joyce Allan wrote another monumental work, interesting and full of information, with many color plates. This was titled *Australian Shells* (Charles E. Branford: Newton Centre, Mass., 1950). It will be many a day before this book is equaled,* and it is probable that both of Joyce Allan's books will be in print for some years to come.

Too many books fall into this group to describe them all here. Some of the choice ones still in print are the following.

There are four shell books from Japan with all plates made up from photographs in excellent color. The text in the regular editions is in Japanese, but the shell names are in Latin, following the custom used universally by scientists. Of these books, all published by Hoikusha (Osaka, Japan), the most useful to own is *Coloured Illustrations of the Shells of Japan,* by Tetsuaki Kira (1962). Useful also are volume 2 in this series, by Tadashige Habe, issued in 1961 under the same title as the Kira volume; *The Trop-*

* *Australian Shells,* by B. R. Wilson and Keith Gillett, was published by the Charles E. Tuttle Co. in 1971, after this book was in press.

ical Pacific, the first volume in the series "Shells of the World in Color"; and another volume in this series, *The Northern Pacific,* by Habe and Ito. The first two books mentioned are also published in larger editions with texts in English. But in my opinion they are overpriced for the slight advantage of larger size and descriptions in English. These *de luxe* editions are available, however, for those who prefer them.

Spencer W. Tinker has written a useful book titled *Pacific Sea Shells* (Charles E. Tuttle: Rutland, Vt., and Tokyo, Japan, 1952), and Percy Morris has written two volumes, with superb photographic plates, some in color, his *Field Guide to the Shells of the Pacific and Hawaii* (Houghton Mifflin: Boston, Mass., 1952) and his 1951 *Field Guide to the Shells of Our Atlantic and Gulf Coasts,* also published by Houghton Mifflin. A masterpiece, and a beautiful book, is *American Seashells* (D. Van Nostrand: Princeton, N.J., 1954), by R. Tucker Abbott. His two inexpensive paperbacks, *How to Know the American Marine Shells* (Signet: New American Library, New York, N.Y., 1961) and *Sea Shells of the World* (Golden Press: New York, N.Y., 1962), have swept the bookstands in department stores and supermarkets.

One of the most intelligently organized and scientifically presented of recent sectional books is Myra Keen's *Sea Shells of Tropical West America* (Stanford University Press: Stanford, Calif., 1958; new enlarged ed., 1972). It shows, for the most part, shells of West Mexico and Panama.

It will be noted that nearly all these books are costly and to own them all would be very expensive. The average collector prefers books which crosscut the world to show those shells most desirable for a personal collection.

The fourth group of books is something of a scintillating explosion. It is composed of a burst of new publications, some extremely expensive, but each one a unique contribution, heralding a great expansion of popular interest in seashells. Oddly enough, some of these books are more concerned with the artistic than the scientific aspect of shells. But even the more technical ones are usually attractive volumes serving not merely as scientific aids but also as side-table picture books. A recent addition to this group is *The Living Cowries* by C. M. Burgess (A. S. Barnes: New York, N.Y., 1970).

Olive Shells of the World, by Porreca and Zeigler (H. C. Porreca: 287 Valley Road, West Henrietta, N.Y., 1969), with thirteen color plates, opens up the obscure world of live shells. Art book of all art books on shells is *The Shell,* by Hugh and Marguerite Stix of New York, husband and wife (Harry N. Abrams: New York, N.Y., 1963). This is a huge tome in which the shape and color of seashells have been exploited to the delight of all viewers.

Even history steps into the picture, for S. Peter Dance has written a fascinating book called *Shell Collecting: An Illustrated History* (University of California Press: Berkeley and Los Angeles, 1966) and its sequel, *Rare Shells* (University of California Press: Berkeley and Los Angeles, 1969), a list of fifty specific shells, and their documented story, but the price is so high that few collectors are likely to own it. Magazine articles like the journalistic story in a recent number of *National Geographic* and a display in the March 1969 number of *Venture Magazine* portray some attractive shells, arbitrarily chosen, in good color. The year 1969 unveiled a very beautiful monthly magazine from Italy, full of photographs, many in superb color. This was *La Conchiglia,* published at Via Tomacelli 146 (IV piano), Rome. At present writing, subscription is about $8.50 a year. No shell fancier who can have this decorative help at his door each month should miss the opportunity to do so.

Now that shells have been so discovered anew there is, and will be, an increasing rush toward new collections. Some of our more wealthy contemporaries are even trifling with shells as a hedge against inflation. With our constant pollution of the seas, and with the new breed of skin divers, there is no doubt that, although the sea will never fail in its riches, rare shells will become rarer as the years go by, as demand exceeds supply. In a few decades I have seen the price of some of them double or triple.

OTHER PUBLICATIONS ABOUT SHELLS

Abbott, R. Tucker (ed.): *Indo-Pacific Mollusca.* Delaware Museum of Natural History: Greenville, Dela. Monographs, 1959-current. Available by subscription.

———: *Kingdom of the Seashell.* Crown Publishers, Inc: New York, N.Y., 1972.

———: *Sea Shells of North America.* Golden Press: New York, N.Y., 1968.

———— and Wagner, Robert J. (eds.): *Standard Catalog of Shells*. D. Van Nostrand: Princeton, N.J., 1967.

Bergeron, Eugene: *How to Clean Sea Shells*. Marine Biological Research Associates: Balboa, Canal Zone, 1966.

Boss, K. J. (ed.): Johnsonia. 4 vols. Museum of Comparative Zoology, Harvard University: Cambridge, Mass. 1941-current.

Carrasco, Herman: *Pre-Colombian Seashells of Mexico*. Lito Offset Perma, S.A.: Mexico, D.F., 1971.

Cernochorsky, Walter O.: *Marine Shells of the Pacific*. Pacific Publications: Sydney, Australia, 1967.

Cox, Ian (ed.): *The Scallop*. Shell Transport and Trading Co.: London, 1957.

Emerson, William K.: *Shells*. Viking Press: New York, N.Y., 1972.

Hawaiian Shell News: 277 Kalakaua Avenue, Honolulu, Hawaii.

Hornell, James: *The Sacred Chank of India*. Madras Fisheries Bulletin 7, 1914. (Out of print.)

Krauss, Helen K.: *Shell Art*. Hearthstone Press: New York, N.Y., 1965.

Kuroda, T., Habe, T., Oyama, K.: *Seashells of Sagami Bay*. Maruzen Co., Ltd.: Tokyo, Japan, 1971. Collection of His Majesty the Emperor of Japan. In color. Text in Japanese and English.

Marsh, A. F. and Rippingale, O. H.: *Cone Shells of the World*. Jacaranda: Brisbane, Australia, 1964.

Melvin, A. Gordon: *Gems of World Oceans*. Naturegraph Publishing Company: Healdsburg, Calif., 1964.

————: *Sea Shells of the World, with Values*. Charles E. Tuttle Co., Inc.: Rutland, Vermont and Tokyo, Japan, 1966.

Merrill, Arthur: *Remarks Concerning the Benefits of Systematic and Repetitive Collecting from Navigation Buoys.* Bureau of Commercial Fisheries: Woods Hole, Mass., 1950.

Smith, Maxwell: *Universal Shells.* Alpine Press: Asheville, N.C., 1961. (Out of print.)

Swainson, William: *Swainson's Exotic Conchology.* D. Van Nostrand: Princeton, N.J., 1963.

Verrill, A. Hyatt: *Shell Collector's Handbook.* G. P. Putnam's Sons: New York, N.Y., 1950.

Weaver, C. C. and duPont, John E.: *The Living Volutes.* Museum of Natural History: Greenville, Dela., 1970.

Webb, Walter Freeman: *Foreign Land Snails.* St. Petersburg, Fla., 1948.

Wilson, B. R. and Gillett, Keith: *Australian Shells.* Charles E. Tuttle Co., Inc.: Rutland, Vermont and Tokyo, Japan, 1970.

75. WHAT IS A SHELL DEALER?

Throughout the earlier years of my life I never heard of a shell dealer. And, although I do not have actual figures, it is my opinion that at the present time not even one person in a hundred is aware that such a being exists, let alone understanding what he does, and why. A shell dealer is usually a person who has extended his interest in shell collecting beyond the hobby stage, and begun to import shells from far countries, selling choice specimens to particular individuals or shell collectors. His business may be a huge concern built into an organized enterprise, like The Shell Factory, in Florida. Or it may be the small personal business of a private individual.

There are not many shell dealers. It is not a lucrative business and must be, in part, a labor of love. While every town or hamlet has its automobile owners, it seems unlikely that more than a third of the cities and towns of the United States have even a single shell collector. In a sense it is the very small size of the individual shell business that allows it to operate as simply and unobtrusively as it does.

Securing first-class specimens from the remote parts of the world is a highly specialized and personalized task, much like a business in jewels. Huge wholesale houses may import sacks and carloads of shells used for craft

74. *Murex pecten* Lightfoot (specimens in perfect to very imperfect condition).

work or for commercial purposes, such as making buttons. But a dealer who supplies the individual collector must not only import in small quantities with heavy postage from many countries, but must struggle to get near-perfect specimens. Each specimen must be inspected, worked over, named, measured, and listed.

The lists must be sent to customers, and when orders come in the shells must be boxed strongly and mailed out. It is a long, tedious, meticulous task. Outside help cannot be used, since the whole process is highly personalized, and most customers are friendly correspondents. The correspondence is tremendous and, although most pleasant, very taxing in terms of time.

Keeping up with changes in prices and in varying supplies of certain specimens, from scarce to plentiful, is very complex indeed. Only the names can be given on lists, and buyers have to know the shell they want by its look or from a picture in a book they have bought. Shells cannot be described with total accuracy in words.

Most shell collectors begin with shells personally secured from beaches they visit. Some collectors are reluctant to buy shells, since they seem to be available virtually free. Yet collectors do learn that certain species can only come from distant lands. Marbled Cone shells all come from the Indo-Pacific seas; Wonder Shells must come from Japan. Emerald Snail shells must come from Manus Island. Golden Cowries usually come from Fiji, and *Cypraea friendi* shells only from West Australia.

The best dealer is one you come to know and trust. A list of select dealers is to be found in *Van Nostrand's Standard Catalog of Shells,* edited by Robert J. Wagner and R. Tucker Abbott (1967). For the rest, you can visit shops that sell seashells in such resort areas as Cape Cod, Massachusetts, and in Florida tourist towns.

In earlier years shell dealers were fewer, but some became famous. One was the Englishman Hugh Fulton (1861–1942); another, also English, was Hugh Berthin Preston (1871–1945), once a tea planter in Ceylon. The American Knight Hadley (1890–1965), of West Newton, a neighbor whom I knew and liked, was for thirty years an important collector and dealer. Walter Freeman Webb, who died a few years ago, was, because of his writings, the most famous shell dealer of his time.

CONCHOLOGY'S
HALL OF FAME

76. THUMBNAIL BIOGRAPHIES

In a sense, every species of shell is personalized. Each species bears the name of a person who described it and gave it its scientific name. One does not work long with shells and their labels before beginning to wonder about the people whose names appear again and again in shell books, and on specimen labels: Linné, Lamarck, Sowerby, Reeve, Philippi, Pilsbry. Unfortunately, records of the lives of most of these men are non-existent or unobtainable. In what follows I have leaned heavily on facts assembled by S. Peter Dance in his 1966 book, *Shell Collecting: An Illustrated History,* a unique work of unexceptionable scholarship essential for anyone interested in the story of shells throughout the centuries.

In what follows I have prepared thumbnail biographies of conchologists whose names appear as the authorities for various species of shells. It includes many whose names are most frequently seen on shell labels, and a few others whose names appear again and again in writings about shells, or under circumstances of special interest. In presenting them I have had to choose between two alternatives, that of giving them in alphabetical order, or offering them in semi-historical sequence. I have chosen the latter because this is the only way in which a reader can get a notion of the historical order in which certain shells were named. Generally speaking, when one sees a person's name on a shell one asks who he was, what country he was from, and how long ago he lived. Only by giving the biographies in some attempt at historical sequence can one be provided with convenient answers to these questions. On the other hand, the most frequent wish of a collector is to satisfy a passing interest in the name of one individual, such as Angas or Hedley.

This latter need should be met quickly, or the moment of interest passes. Consequently I have preceded the biographies with an alphabetical list of names, each name being followed by a key number for immediate reference to the biographies. In this way, I hope, both the need for historical reference and the satisfaction of immediate curiosity will be simply met.

Here, then, is the alphabetical list, with key numbers to be used in finding the biographies which follow:

A long and unique list of about two hundred men who have given names to shells is to be found in Webb's *Handbook for Shell Collectors*. Although supplementary to what has been given here, the list gives names and country of origin only, and does not include biographical material or dates.

I should like to continue the series of brief biographies presented above to include a number of people who have contributed to new knowledge in this century. Unfortunately such biographical material is unavailable, and any attempt to secure it would delay publication of this book. I shall merely, therefore, append the names of a number of people whose biographies I should like to add. If any friends or relatives of the men listed are able to write me, care of the publisher, providing me with names, dates, anecdotes, and biographical material, I shall try, in later writing, to make what I have written here more complete, and so preserve some historical record of the workers of this century. Among those whom I would select to report on are the following, in alphabetical order:

Abbott, R. Tucker, U.S.A.
Bartsch, Paul, U.S.A.
Bednall, W. T., Australia
Berry, S. Stillman, U.S.A.
Cate, Crawford N., U.S.A.
Clench, William J., U.S.A.
Dall, W. H., U.S.A.
Emerson, William K., U.S.A.
Eschcholtz, Dr., Germany
Habe, Tadashige, Japan
Hanna, D. W., U.S.A.
Hartman, D. W., U.S.A.
Iredale, Tom, Australia
Jeffreys, J. Gwyn, England
Kira, Tetsuaki, Japan
Lischke, C. E., Germany
Pease, William Harper, U.S.A.
Powell, A. W. Baden, New Zealand
Redfield, John, U.S.A.
Rehder, Harold A., U.S.A.
Schilder, Franz Alfred, Germany
Souverbie, Dr., France
Strong, A. M., U.S.A.
Thiele, Prof. Johannes, Germany
Torres, Carlos de la, Cuba
Turner, Ruth, U.S.A.
Turton, W. H., England

These conchologists worked with shells before Linnaeus introduced the system of binomial nomenclature (first name for the genus, second name for the individual shell, or the species).

1. **Buonani, Philippe** (1638–1725): Italian Jesuit, pre-Linnaean naturalist who wrote *Recreatione dell' Occhio e della Mante,* a picture book of mollusks. This was the first modern publication of any size on shells. Buonani was a man ahead of his time.

2. **Lister, Dr. Martin** (1638–1712): Physician to Queen Anne of England. One of the pre-Linnaean naturalists, he wrote *Historia Conchyliorum* (1685–1692). The book had nearly a thousand plates picturing shells.

3. **Rumphius, Georg Eberhard** (1627–1702): Dutch pre-Linnaean naturalist. (His Dutch name was Rumph.) A contemporary of Dr. Lister, he spent a large part of his life on the island of Amboina, in the employ of the Dutch East India Company. Although Rumphius was pre-Linnaean, Linnaeus later on adopted some of his names for shells; some of these names, for example *Tellina virgata* L., remain in use.

CONCHOLOGISTS OF THE 1700'S:
LINNAEUS AND OTHERS

4. **Meuschen, Friedrich Christian** (1719?–1800): Dutch shell dealer who catalogued several important collections. His name still remains as authority for a number of species, *Ancilla torosa* Meuschen, for example.

5. **Linnaeus, Carl (Carl von Linné; 1707–1778)**: Swedish genius who applied the binomial system to all animals and plants, thus making the science of biology possible. According to his system each entity has two names, the first that of the genus (group), the second that of the species, a particular name applied only to that individual type.

In his *Systema Naturae* he described every animal he knew, and gave it a name. Many of these names still persist, although many have been changed. The binomial system itself, however, remains the indispensable tool of the natural sciences. His picture appears in S. Peter Dance's 1966 book, *Shell Collecting: An Illustrated History*.

6. **Bolten, Johann Friedrich (1718–1796)**: German contemporary of Linnaeus. A prominent physician in Hamburg, his collection of gastropods contained 7,000 shells. Certain shells still bear his name as their authority.

7. **Lightfoot, Rev. John (1735–1788)**: Englishman, chaplain to the duchess of Portland. He drew up the *Portland Catalogue* for the sale of her famous shell collection. His name appears as authority for *Voluta imperialis* Lightfoot.

8. **Adanson, Michel (1727–1806)**: French contemporary of Linnaeus; pioneering naturalist who collected plants and animals in Senegal. His *Histoire Naturelle de Sénégal* was a study of molluskan life. He was the first naturalist who consistently used a binomial system of naming. In a sense, he was the first to treat conchology as a science. His name appears on *Conus adansonii* Lam., now said to be synonymous with *C. mediterraneus*.

9. **Cracherode, Rev. Clayton Mordaunt (1730–1799)**: Englishman, the first to give an important collection of shells to the British Museum, that great repository of

shells. For many of his specimens he paid very high prices. His name appears on *Haliotis cracherodi* Leach.

10. **Chemnitz, Rev. Johann Hieronymus** (1730–1800): Danish collector who at first collected cut shells, but later whole ones. He continued *Conchylien-cabinet,* a work significant because of its many illustrations, begun by the Hamburg physician-naturalist Friedrich Wilhelm Martini (1729–1778) but interrupted by his death. Chemnitz also wrote up the chitons. He has received more than his share of attention because he named *Conus gloriamaris* Chemnitz.

11. **Hwass, Christian Hee** (1731–1803): Dane who lived his later life in France. He was a wealthy collector who owned many rare shells, including specimens of the Golden Cowry and *Conus gloriamaris*. His collection is now in the Natural History Museum of Geneva. In a monograph he wrote on cones, many of them received the names they now carry, although these names are regarded as controversial by some.

There is a story that Hwass, on receiving a second specimen of a very rare shell, smashed it to pieces so he would be the owner of the only known specimen. Of course one need not credit this unlikely tale.

12. **Gmelin, Johann Friedrich** (1748–1804): English naturalist who wrote an important work, *Caroli a Linne Systema Naturae per Regna Naturae*. He was the nephew of the naturalist and traveler Johann Georg Gmelin (1700–1755) and father of the chemist Leopold Gmelin (1788–1853). His name is frequently seen as the authority for the names of many shells.

LAMARCK AND OTHERS

13. **Lamarck, chevalier de** (title of **Jean Baptiste Pierre**

Antoine de Monet, 1774–1829): French naturalist, the second great figure in the world of molluskan nomenclature. A professor of zoology in the Natural History Museum of Paris, he amassed an important collection which he used in preparing his written works.

The British followers of Linnaeus violently opposed the changes in the Linnaean system proposed by Lamarck, but both systems have made their mark on subsequent science. The two systems are superbly outlined, in basic form, on insets in the rare volume *A Conchological Manual,* by J. B. Sowerby, Jr., *ca.* 1852.

14. **Martyn, Thomas** (*ca.* 1789): Englishman who, by dint of training a group of young artists, was able to publish his *Universal Conchologist.* He spent a large part of his personal fortune to produce this masterpiece, which is not regarded as binomial.

15. **Sowerby, James** (1757–1822): Englishman, first of the four Sowerbys. An artist and biologist of ability, he began in 1821 to publish his *Genera of Recent Fossil Shells.* The illustrations showed specimens of Lamarckian genera, and were accompanied by annotations. After his death his son G. B. Sowerby continued his unfinished work.

16. **Dufresne, Louis** (1752–1832): French collector whose name appears on *Voluta dufresnei* Donovan.

17. **Schumacher, Dr. Christian Frederick** (1757–1830): German medical doctor, friend of Hwass and Lamarck. He is responsible for certain names such as *Rapana* and *Gari.*

18. **Smith, John Edward** (1759–1828): Englishman, purchaser of the Linnaean shell collection. He became famous and was knighted in 1814. He was one of the founders of the Linnaean Society of London.

19. **Montfort, Denys de** (d. *ca.* 1821): French author of the first four volumes of *Histoire Naturelle . . . de Mollusques,* and two volumes of *Conchyliologie Systematique.* He supplied such familiar names as *Magilus, Phos, Trophon,* and *Capulus.* In the end, it is said, he starved to death in the streets of Paris.

20. **Mawe, John** (1764–1829): English author of *The Linnaean System of Conchology* (1825). He sailed the seas of the world for fifteen years. While traveling in South America he was held prisoner in Montevideo. He opened a shop at 149 The Strand, in London, where he sold natural history specimens, including shells. His name appears on the fantastically shaped *Latiaxis mawae* Griffith & Pidgeon.

21. **Adams, John** (1767–1829): Englishman, last survivor on Pitcairn Island of the mutineers of the *Bounty.* Cuming (see 26, below) visited him on that island on the last stop of his Polynesian collecting trip, from which he arrived in Valparaiso, Chile, in 1828.

22. **Link, Heinrich Friedrich** (1767–1851): German author who gave names to genera, such as *Phalium.* His name appears on a favorite shell, *Lambis crocata* Link, displacing the later name, *Pterocera aurantia* Lam.

23. **Duclos, F. L.** (d. *ca.* 1853): French collector who owned over twenty thousand specimens of cowries. He studied a number of shells which now bear his name as their authority.

24. **Hinds, Richard Brinsley** (d. *ca.* 1858): Englishman who participated in the work of describing Cuming's shells. As ship's surgeon on the voyage of the *Sulphur* (1836–1858) under Captain Belcher he collected many shells, some of which he described and named, including some neglected genera of small shells.

25. **Perry, George** (*ca.* 1860): Englishman, a much maligned, controversial figure. His odd book *Conchology* (1816) is today almost priceless. In spite of opposition to his unorthodox procedures, some of his names remain intact, among them *Biplex* and *Hexaplex,* now used to classify the *Murex* family.

CUMING, HIS ASSOCIATES, AND OTHER GIANTS

26. **Cuming, Hugh** (1791–1865): Englishman, the greatest shell collector of all time. Cuming early settled as a sail-maker in Buenos Aires. He soon had a large shell collection, a daughter, Valentina, a son, Hugh Valentine, and, incidentally, a mistress, Mona de los Santos.

   He retired from business at the early age of 35. He then began a series of astonishing voyages throughout Polynesia, South America, and the Philippines, amassing the greatest collection ever known. With these freshly gathered shells, he fed the scientific studies of the Sowerbys and of Lovell Reeve. His stupendous collection was bought by the British Museum for £6,000, and it there resides.

27. **Wood, William** (1774–1857): Englishman who wrote a popular book on shells, *General Conchology,* in which he followed the Linnaean system. His name appears on several species of American West Coast shells, for example *Astraea undosa* Wood. Generally speaking, he sided with proponents of the Linnaean system.

28. **Adamson, John** (1787–1855): English collector whose name is given to the rare shell *Conus adamsoni* Broderip, the synonym of which is *Conus rhododendron* Jay.

29. **Sowerby, George Brettingham** (1788–1854): English-

man. Sowerby was the second of his name to concern himself with shells. He carried on the work of his father, James Sowerby, portraying shells of the Lamarckian genera. He bought the famous collection of the earl of Tankerville, and in the same year, the huge stock of the London dealer George Humphrey. After he had spent about six thousand pounds in this way, the import duty on shells was repealed by the government. As a result, shells inundated the market; this caused a drop in prices and considerable loss to Sowerby.

The name Sowerby appears with frequency as the authority for many shells, but now it is difficult to tell which of the Sowerbys actually named which shells. The name Sowerby, on a shell, seems merely to indicate one or another member of the dynasty. In 1842 the first G. B. Sowerby published the first section of *Thesaurus Conchyliorum*. The five volumes, with many superb plates, took three generations of Sowerbys—altogether forty-five years—to complete, and some of the subscribers died before receiving the entire *Thesaurus*.

30. Swainson, William (1789–1855): Englishman, another of the towering figures in conchology. Swainson spent years in the Mediterranean, in the British army. He also visited South America. Naturalist, artist, and author, he wrote *Swainson's Exotic Conchology*, a notable work, with colored plates. Emigrating to New Zealand, he spent the last part of his life there. His biography, with portrait, is to be seen in a facsimile reproduction of *Exotic Conchology* published in 1963.

31. Broderip, William John (1789–1859): Englishman; London magistrate, born in Bristol. As a child he played with shells in his father's collection. He was wealthy, and made a fine collection of his own, which included the excessively rare *Cypraea valentia, Cypraea guttata, Cypraea leucodon,* and *Conus gloriamaris.* The collection was sold to the British Museum in 1837, for £1,575. Some of Swainson's illustrations were drawings of Broderip's shells.

In this period many world voyages took place. As a result, many species never observed before were brought in, requiring study by numerous new workers in the field of conchology. Identification went on apace.

32. **Quoy, Jean René Constant** (1790–1858): French naturalist, who sailed in that capacity on the voyages of the *Uranie* (*ca.* 1800) and the *Physicienne* (*ca.* 1820). Together with Gaimard he sailed around the world in the *Astrolabe* between 1826 and 1829, making collections. The rare split shell *Perotrochus quoyana* Fischer & Bernardi bears his name. With Gaimard he named a number of shells.

33. **Orbigny, Alcide Dessalines d'** (1802–1857): Frenchman. When he was twenty-four years old, under the auspices of the Natural History Museum of Paris, he traveled for six years in Brazil, Argentina, Bolivia, Chile, and Peru.

    The fifth volume of his *Voyage dans l'Amérique Méridionale* has many colored plates of shells, making it still the most comprehensive account of mollusks of South America. D'Orbigny also described many shells gathered by Ramon de la Sagra in Cuba, and others collected by Philip Barker Webb in the Canary Islands.

34. **Couthouy, John Pilly** (1808–1864): American, conchologist of the Scientific Corps, Couthouy was the first

to go on a voyage sponsored by the U.S. government for the purpose of collecting mollusks. His collection was damaged by careless handling in Washington. Ultimately it reached A. A. Gould (see 38, below), who published a report on it.

35. **Gray, John Edward** (1800–1875): Englishman, one-time assistant in the British Museum. He described some of Cuming's shells.

36. **Reeve, Lovell Augustus** (1814–1865): Englishman. A grocer's apprentice, at the age of thirteen he became fascinated with shells when a sailor brought in a handkerchief of cowries.

   He became a dealer in shells and a publisher of books at his London shop. The lithographed plates in his great twenty-volume *Conchologica Iconica* were a triumph. In preparing it he used many shells of the Cuming collection. He was a beneficiary under Cuming's will. As every collector probably soon finds out, Reeve is the authority for the names of very many shells. His photograph also appears in Dance's *Shell Collecting*.

37. **Deshayes, Gerard Paul** (1796–1875): French conchological author who, with Henri Milne-Edwards, edited the second and third editions of Lamarck's *Histoire Naturelle des Animaux sans Vertèbres*. He also wrote on the history of conchology, and gave names to many shells.

38. **Gould, Augustus Addinson** (1805–1866): American author of a number of books and papers on mollusks. He wrote the first American shell manual, *The Conchologist*. His name appears as authority for many species of American West Coast shells.

39. **Adams, Charles Baker** (1814–1853): American, professor of zoology at Amherst College, Massachusetts. He

was considered to have had the most valuable collection, for study, in the United States at that time. In 1847, Adams issued a catalog of his collection listing 1,773 species, mostly from Panama and Jamaica, some of which he had himself collected and named.

40. Valenciennes, Achille (*ca.* 1830): He described many shells brought back by the German explorer-collector Alexander von Humboldt (1769–1850) from the western coasts of Peru and Mexico. He also directed the publication of twenty-four superb plates, showing about eighty species collected in the Indo-Pacific and on the western coasts of the Americas during the voyage of the *Venus,* commanded by A. duPetit Thouars.

41. Blainville, H. M. de (*ca.* 1830): French authority for certain species of shells. He introduced the word *malacology*, first proposed by Rafinesque, in his *Manuel de Malacologie*.

42. Delessert, Baron J.P.B. (*ca.* 1840): French collector who was said to have had the largest collection ever assembled in France. He was an associate of Kiener and Chenu. His name appears in *Voluta delessertiana* Petit.

43. Kiener, Louis Charles (1799–1881): Frenchman who named many shells in a long career during which he had available the collection of the French Baron Delessert, as well as the shells in the Natural History Museum of Paris.

Ten volumes of his illustrated *Spécies Général et Iconographie des Coquilles Vivantes* dealt with mollusks. The shells in his works are said to have been modified in form and color by artistic "improvements," in contrast to the objective accuracy of shells portrayed by British illustrators.

44. Thouars, A. du Petit (*ca.* 1840): Frenchman, captain of the *Venus,* which sailed around the world 1836–1839. He collected over fifteen hundred mollusks on the voyage. The shells were shown on twenty-four plates prepared with the help of Valenciennes and published without the accompanying text. His name appears on the West Mexican shell *Fusus dupetit-thouarsi* Kiener.

45. **Küster, Heinrich Carl** (1807–1876): German worker who edited an enlarged edition of *Conchylien-cabinet,* by Martini and Chemnitz. Although it is large in bulk, this work suffers from inferior illustrations and out-of-date informative material.

46. **Bernardi, A.** (d. 1863): French conchologist who named certain species. He assisted Cross with the *Journal de Conchyliologie*.

47. **Pfeiffer, Louis** (1815–1877): German, famed prolific author, and specialist on land shells. He described many of Cuming's shells.

48. **Dunker, Rudolf Wilhelm** (1809–1885): German who described and named some of Cuming's shells.

49. **Say, Thomas** (1787–1834): American, pioneer conchologist whose name appears as authority for a number of shells. His portrait is to be seen in Maxwell Smith's *Universal Shells* (1961).

50. **Sowerby, George Brettingham, Jr.** (1812–1884): Englishman; a lesser light than his father, but an excellent artist. At the age of twenty, with his father's help, he issued the first number of *The Conchological Illustrations,* which took nine years to complete.

Another significant contribution was his editing, after Reeve's death, of the last five volumes of the twenty-volume *Conchologica Iconica*. He also published a *Conchological Manual* which went through four editions.

George Brettingham Sowerby 3rd carried on his father's business in shells from 1892–1897, when he entered into partnership with the dealer H. C. Fulton.

51. Carpenter, Rev. Philip Pearsall (1819–1877): English-man. He made a report on the large collection of shells of Mazatlan, Mexico, gathered by the Belgian Frederick Reigen. He also described a number of Cuming's shells.

52. Adams, Anthony (1820–1878): Englishman whose name is often seen, as he described hundreds of new shells. (Many of them were Cuming's.) He observed and sketched many living mollusks. With Reeve he made a report, with his own illustrations, of shells obtained on the voyage of the *Samarang* (1843–1846) on which he served as a surgeon, sailing widely in Indonesian waters.

53. Milne-Edwards, Henri (*ca.* 1850): French concholo-gist who assisted Deshayes in editing the second and third editions of Lamarck's *Histoire Naturelle des Animaux sans Vertèbres*. His name was attached to the rare shell *Conus milne-edwardsi* Jousseaume.

THE MID-1800's TO 1900: WORLD HORIZONS

54. Stainforth, Rev. F. J. (d. 1869): English collector who furnished Reeve with specimens for his illustrations, whereupon Reeve gave his name to several shells such as *Murex stainforthi* Reeve.

At one time he owned the specimen of *Conus gloria-maris* Chemnitz which Reeve used as a model for the engraving on the frontispiece in his *Conchologica Iconica*. It is reproduced in Dance's *Shell Collecting*.

55. Mörch, Otto Andreas Lowson (1828–1878): Danish conchologist who catalogued several important collections, one of which he recorded in the *Yoldi Catalogue*. In the process of his work he named a number of new species.

56. **Dillwyn, Lewis Weston** (1778–1885): English author of the manual *Descriptive Catalogue of Recent Shells*. His name appears as authority for a number of shells.

57. **Philippi, Rudolf Amandus** (1808–1904): German conchologist who named some well-known shells. He published a useful set of illustrated monographs.

58. **Hanley, Charles Thorp** (1819–1899): Englishman who described some of Cuming's shells. An indefatigable writer and special authority on bivalves, he wrote *The Young Conchologist's Book of Species* and other studies.

59. **Angas, George French** (1822–1886): English contemporary of Cuming, Reeve, and Sowerby. He named that great favorite among shells, *Thatcheria mirabilis* Angas.

60. **Melvill, James Cosmo** (*ca.* 1845): English collector who described many shells. He wrote a description of Hugh Cuming as he saw him at the sale of the celebrated Dennison Collection.

61. **Crosse, Joseph Charles Hippolyte** (1826–1898): French lawyer. His lifelong interest in conchology developed from his fascination with a collection of shells he was given at the age of fifteen.

62. **Martens, Carl Eduard von** (1831–1904): German. He was the leading conchologist of his time in his country, and a curator of the Berlin Zoological Museum. He sailed as a naturalist on the voyage of the *Thetis* (1860), visiting China and Japan, and later Sumatra, Java, and the Moluccas. He described many shells, among them many land shells.

63. **Röding, Peter Freidrich** (1767–1846): German. He wrote *The Bolten Catalogue,* which became very significant in providing acceptable names for many shells. He supplied synonyms and references to published illustrations of Bolten's collection, thus fulfilling the requirements for the proper naming of shells. The Röding names were brought to light, over fifty years later, by William Healey (1845–1927). Consternation ensued because some of Lamarck's names, such as *Rostellaria, Pterocera,* and *Melania,* had to be dropped.

64. **Cox, James Charles** (1833–1912): Australian. His collection included such rare shells as *Conus gloriamaris* Chemnitz and *Cypraea valentia* Perry, which was auctioned in London in 1905. His name appears on the odd little cowry *Cypraea coxeni* Cox.

65. **Fischer, Paul** (1835–1893): French conchologist, who prepared the eleventh volume of Kiener's *Spécies Général et Iconographie des Coquilles Vivantes,* and also aided Crosse and Bernardi in reviving the *Journal de Conchyliologie.* As authority, his name appears on the rare *Perotrochus quoyana* Fischer & Bernardi.

66. **Dohrn, Heinrich** (1838–1913): German, owner of the largest shell collection of his time in Germany. This was enlarged by the addition of the shells of three important collections, those of L. Pfeiffer, Eduard Romer, and Franz Troschel. The total collection was destroyed in World War II. Dohrn named many new shell species.

67. **Smith, Edgar Albert** (1847–1916): English authority for a considerable number of shell species. For some years he looked after Cuming's shells, and gradually became an authority on mollusks. He stoutly defended Cuming against his detractors.

68. Hidalgo, Joaquin Gonzalez (1843–1923): Spaniard, professor of malacology at the University of Madrid. He amassed a fine collection, later placed in the Museum of Natural Sciences in Madrid. He wrote on the shells of Spain, Portugal, the Balearic Islands, and the Philippines. Some shells from western Mexico were named by him.

69. Brazier, John (1842–1930): Australian contemporary of Hedley. He was active in writing papers on shells which awakened Australian enthusiasm for collecting. His name, as authority, appears on some shells.

70. Dautzenberg, Philippe (1849–1935): Belgian collector who inherited a fortune from a family business in carpeting. He is reported to have had thirty thousand species, including the rare *Cypraea venusta* Sowerby, and *Cypraea valentia* Perry. He is the authority for the names of several species of shells.

71. Verco, Dr. (Sir Joseph; 1851–1933): Australian who wrote an account of his dredging excursions on the south and west coasts of Australia in his book *Combing the Southern Sea* (1935). This did much to stimulate the great expansion of collecting by Australians.

72. Hedley, Charles (1862–1926): He named some shells, and by writing his scientific papers helped to awaken Australian interest in shell collecting.

73. Tryon, George Washington (1838–1888): American. He was a wealthy resident of Philadelphia who planned his *Manual of Conchology* on such a grand scale that he died before it was half completed. It was carried on by Pilsbry, his successor as Conservator of the Conchological Section of the Philadelphia Academy.

74. Pilsbry, Henry Augustus (1862–1957): American who

became the successor to Tryon in the Philadelphia Academy. In this post he spent a life of diligent work on shells. He provided over 5,600 new names, it has been estimated, in the field of malacology.

75. Hirase, Yoichiro (1859–1925): Japanese, great forerunner of Japanese malacology. Although shells have appeared in Japanese art for centuries, it remained for a wealthy gentleman, Yoichiro Hirase, to respond to the impact of Western science by laying the foundation for the superb work of the Japanese in malacology.

He made his lifetime work collecting and studying 3,500 species, many of which were not previously known to science. Many of these he described himself, and they now bear his name.

INDEX

Photographs of most of the shells indexed, but not illustrated in this book, may be seen in the author's *Seashells of the World*. Numbers in italic indicate pages on which illustrations appear.

Ovula ovum   223

Packing shells   319, *320*, 321–22

Padre Island   270, 272–73; map of, 271

Pahl, Ronald   88, 90

Panther Cowry. *See* Cypraea pantherina

Paper Nautilus   24, 58, *59*, 60–61, 296

Papuina pulcherrima   74, *75*, 76–77, 194

Pastry Shell. *See* Callanaitis disjecta

Patterns on shells   172, 174, 175

Peace Miter. *See* Mitra zaca

Pearls, from mussels   194

Pecten irradians   142, *143*, 144–45

Pecten jacobeus   42, *43*, 44–46

Pecten magellanicus   142, *143*, 224, 253

Pecten nobilis   *189*, 192, 194

Pecten nodosus   *193*, 194

Pecten yessoensis   224

Peking   176, 178

Periwinkle   105, *106*, 107–8, 260

Perotrochus hirasei   47, *48*, 49, 224, 228, *229*, 305

Philadelphia Museum of Natural Sciences   313

Phyopsis africanum   *151*, 153

Pinctada mazatlanica   *67*, 68–69

Pink-Mouthed Murex. *See* Murex erythrostoma

Pink Murex. *See* Murex bicolor

Pink Roller. *See* Strombus gigas

Placuna ephippium. *See* Placuna sella

Placuna placenta   196, *197*, 198–99

Placuna sella   196, 198

Plate Limpet. *See* Acmaea testudinalis

Pleuroploca gigantea   135

Pleurotomaria hirasei   *See* Perotrochus hirasei

Poisonous cones   88, *89*, 90, 91

Polimita picta   111

Polinices duplicatus   208

Pontifical Miter. *See* Mitra pontificalis

Pope's Miter. *See* Mitra papalis

Postage Stamps   228, *229*, 230–31

Pottery-ware   232, *233*, 234

Precious Wentletrap   70, *71*, 72–73

Prelate Cone. *See* Conus praelatus

Prieto, Carlos   294, 296, 304

Pterocera aurantia   160

Puerto Marques, Mexico   66, 104, 278, *279*

Purple dye   140–41

Purpura patula   141

Quahog Clams. *See* Venus mercenaria

366